Boho
EMBROIDERY

Modern Projects from
Traditional Stitches

NICHOLE VOGELSINGER

Published in 2016 by Lucky Spool Media,
LLC
www.luckyspool.com
info@luckyspool.com

Text © Nichole Vogelsinger
Editor: Susanne Woods
Designer: Rae Ann Spitzenberger
Illustrator: Kari Vojtechovsky
Embroidery Illustrator: Alison Glass
Water Color Artist: Cindy Derby
Photographer: Holly DeGroot

Photograph on page 12
© Sam Gehring
Photograph on page 86
© Bill Bachhuber

9 8 7 6 5 4 3 2 1
First Edition
Printed in China

Library of Congress Cataloging-in-
Publication Data available upon request
ISBN 978-1-940655-20-8
LSID0033

CONTENTS

DEDICATION

I hereby dedicate any past, present, and future comma splices to Bix aka The Grammar Nerd.

To Brett for your (mostly) rationale words of wisdom in helping me to stay (mostly) sane and for your unwavering support ... "and a whole lotta love." Thank you for binge watching Netflix with me so that I could stitch deep into the night! To Leo, for your positivity and cheer and chatter. ILY. To Remy, my sidekick, for your creativity and color-matching skills. Aloha. And mostly, for (all of your) patience and love.

To Sir and Mom, who have been so supportive and loving and ready to help whenever (and however!) I needed it. I love you both so much!

To Danielle for your gypsy awesomeness. To Nicci for your linguistic enthusiasm. To Renee for being in the circle of trust. To Meg for your advice on all things wordsmithery (that's totally a word!). To Jade, Shannon, and Rhea for helping me to be Superwoman!

To Guinevere, Ava, Gisele and Elliot for being the best cold-weather denim models a girl could ask for!

ACKNOWLEDGMENTS

To the Instagram community for all of the hoop-love! I could not have found a better space to share my creativity and receive such a kind reception. And a special thanks to the fellow artists and designers whom I have virtually met and whom I continue to be inspired by.

To Daryl and Giuseppe at Andover Fabrics for your cheerleading and hoop-ing opportunities. Oh, and fabric! For all of the fabric!

To Kelly, my thread guru at Sue Spargo for introducing me to and providing me with many of the threads I used for projects throughout this book.

To Susanne and Lucky Spool for allowing me the opportunity to write about something I love. Not everyone has the chance for their work to be creatively inspiring — and for that chance, I am so appreciative.

To a brilliant creative team...this book is everything that I hoped it would be! To Holly for your amazing style sense and photography! To Alison, Kari and Cindy for blending your individual artistic talents to create something so seamless! To Rae Ann for your design skills! To Shea and Lisa and Deanna for all of the behind-the-scenes work that you did to help me get to this point. I can't thank you all enough!

INTRODUCTION
let's talk about boho embroidery

You'll meet many crafters, and perhaps you are one yourself, who took to stitching or sewing or quilting almost immediately in life. It is a skill they somehow just knew they possessed. When others their age were sporting around with a ball and bat or lazing away their summer days listening to music and hanging out with friends, they deftly wielded a needle and thread. I am not one of those people.

My mother is a fabulous seamstress. As a child, I watched her smock dresses by hand for my sister and me in what seemed like no time at all. She tried her best to help me sew, but all I could manage was to jam up her trusty Singer with a mess of thread. She was able to teach others how to sew and quilt, and did so at our local fabric store, but she could not teach me. I gave up machine sewing at the ripe old age of about ten and somewhere, dusty in an attic, sits my little machine, still jammed with thread.

Despite my early failures with a sewing machine, I still felt the urge to craft. So I experimented with things that weren't machine-based: macramé and embroidery floss friendship bracelets and then moving into rug hooking, cross-stitch and knitting. And Friendly Plastic ... does anyone else remember spending afternoons cutting pieces of hard plastic and melting them in hot water on the stove to create barrettes and pendants and pins? Doing those handcrafts was how I discovered I did actually have some creative bones in my body, and that is how I crafted away my teens and early twenties.

It wasn't until a few years ago, when I had my first son, that I felt the urge to pull out my mother's old machine, which she handed down to me in hopes that I would someday get the sewing bug, and give the whole sewing thing a go once again My first project was a small throw rug that I pieced together while I watched Duchess Kate get married on the television in the background. I learned that I could actually operate a sewing machine without jamming it into an inoperable state! A fabric-filled new world was opened to me just as surface designers were releasing incredible fabric lines like never before. Oh, the fabric!

Living in a house built in the early 1900s, charming as it can be, leaves me with small rooms without closets. Storage for these dearly loved fabrics is always at a premium. I wanted to see the fabrics that I loved, rather than just stashing them away in a drawer somewhere, and so I decided that I needed to create art using those beloved fabrics.

Embroidery hoop art was in its early stages of becoming a trendy way to decorate. When I made my first few hoops and posted pictures of them on Instagram, people asked me, "What are you supposed to do with them?" Soon, though, hoop art was seen everywhere, and it was exciting to be part of the growth in this form of textile art. What differentiated my hoops, the ones you are going to learn how to make in this book, were the layers of fabric with

embroidered stitches embellishing parts of the fabric. This look was created so that I could see several of my favorite fabrics at once, because, remember, I was determined not to be a mere fabric collector!

If you have precious bits of fabric that you want to see rather than store away, then this is the textile art to explore! I hope that the hoops you see pictured and described throughout will visually inspire creativity, and the projects you make will add color and pattern and texture to your home. Pattern and color can sometimes seem overwhelming, but hoop art is a small way to begin experimenting with it and will

help you develop confidence in mixing and matching both.

Once you feel you have mastered the basic embroidery and appliqué techniques, you will be able to think "outside the hoop," discovering new applications for these skills. A vintage or secondhand shirt can be made one-of-a-kind. A handmade clutch can become even more personalized with your added details. Clothing, whether handmade or bought, can be personalized with these techniques.

Whether you are an old hand with a needle and thread or this is a new craft to you and you don't have a box of jumbled up floss stored somewhere in your crafting supplies, you will learn fun techniques and find new inspiration that will give you the jumping off point to create something fresh and modern. And soon you'll have a jumbled box of floss to call your very own!

WHAT IS BOHO?

So what exactly is "Boho Embroidery?" How about if we start with what Boho embroidery is not? Boho embroidery is not stitching a printed needlepoint sampler while listening to Joni Mitchell with sandalwood incense burning in the background. Although, if that's your thing, you should definitely go with that...I'm all for stitching along with "Ladies of the Canyon" playing in the background. Boho embroidery is not about following specific rules and yet it's not about breaking them either. It's not about counting stitches or following patterns. You do need to know the basics of the embroidery

stitches taught here. But it is about forging your own way.

Once you have learned several hand embroidery stitches, you will have the freedom to wander down your own creative path and create something that is uniquely yours. This book does not include patterns that will allow you to create a piece exactly like that which I have shown in an example. I encourage you to take the patterns that are included and make them your own. Use them as a base for your own art. Challenge yourself to be different, to be unique, to encompass the free-spiritedness that Boho embroidery has to offer! Use the inspiration included throughout to push yourself creatively. Choose a variety of fabrics and textures and threads. Allow yourself to step outside of the hoop and incorporate your new skills into other crafty areas of your life.

Now, let's get started, shall we?

CHAPTER 1

✗ ✗ ✗ ✗ ✗ ✗ ✗ ✗ ✗ ✗

Let's Talk About

TOOLS

Hand embroidery is one of the most portable crafts. After all, you do not need much more than your current project, a needle (or two, because I cannot trust myself not to lose one while on the go!), scissors, and thread. Pack it all up in a sturdy container, and you are ready to go. I like to use an ArtBin; the hard plastic keeps my project safe and the convenient handle is a plus when traveling.

This is also a craft that can be picked up and put down as needed. It is not like counted cross-stitch, where you are following a pattern and need to keep track of where you are. It does not require a sewing machine; although, if you have one, it allows you to mix and match fabrics differently. A machine is not needed for any project in this book.

It is the ideal group craft. Host a small group and swap materials and ideas. Crafting today can be a collaborative effort, much like the crazy quilting swaps and parties of the Victorian era, where women would gather together to work on the same kind of project. Or even before, quilting bees where women would come together to work on the quilting of a large project. These bees would sometimes take place in the course of an entire day and would end with a party-like gathering with food and games and entire families would attend.

It seems like a scene straight out of Little House on the Prairie, doesn't it? But the unique bond that forms from artistically working together and sharing ideas is timeless.

So, let's talk about tools!

MUST HAVES
» Hoop
» Variety of Needles
» Microtip Scissors
» Variety of Threads
» Several Fabrics
» HeatnBond
» Marking Tools
» Adhesives
» Light Source

let's talk thread

If you are new to the colorful world of thread, then this will help you to determine what you are looking for when you choose the thread for your first project. You will oftentimes hear "embroidery floss" and "thread" or "embroidery thread" used interchangeably. Do not be confused: they are all basically the same thing. The term used just depends on what part of the world you are crafting in! What you do need to pay close attention to is what ply, or strand, you are looking for. The two plys you will most likely see are single strand and six strand. Perle cottons, like Eleganza, and specialty threads, like Cosmo Nishiikito and Sue Spargo's Razzle and Dazzle, are made of just one strand that you do not separate. Regular embroidery floss, like Aurifloss, Cosmo or DMC, is sold in six strand

skeins that can either be used as all six strands together or they can be separated to whatever weight you want.

When you are ready to use your first spool or skein of thread, begin by cutting a workable (for you) length. There is no right or wrong length, the length you use is based on your preference.

To knot or not to knot...that is the question. Again, this is completely up to you! I like to tie a small knot at the end of my cut length of thread and then thread the unknotted end through the needle. Some stitchers do not like to tie any knots. Either way you decide to go, it will not make a noticeable difference in your work, so do what you like!

Now, let's talk about types of thread before we move on!

"What is the difference between DMC floss and specialty floss?" If you are part of the crafting world, you will have either asked yourself that question or you will have seen discussions about it online. Inquiring minds want to know! It can be hard to see the difference for yourself, because these threads, while easy to buy online, cannot all be found in brick and mortar stores. You may want to try different threads, but are hesitant to spend the money without knowing if you will like them. Well, read on. To make it easier for you (especially if you are a newbie), I have selected my very favorite threads and explained the differences between them so you can evaluate the pros and cons yourself and decide which threads you want to try.

DMC FLOSS

If you need embroidery floss and you need it fast, this is the brand for you. DMC floss is available in nearly every fabric and craft store. Because it is so easy to find, it is the thread that most crafters are familiar with. It is also the least expensive thread. At 40¢–50¢ a skein, it is easy to go in the store looking for a handful of colors and end up going home with more than you will probably ever use! Just try to resist all the colors!

DMC boasts an impressive array of more than 450 colors. It is also available in several varieties: cotton floss, pearl cotton skeins, pearl cotton balls, color variations, metallic, light effects, linen and satin.

note: Most of these varieties, except for the perle cotton and metallic, come in skeins of six strands. You can use all six together or you can separate them depending on the look you want. For most of my projects, I use four strands, because I like my stitches to be noticeable and feel substantial while I am stitching. To stitch tiny details, like faces, I typically use just two strands together. This really is a personal preference, though, so practice with the threads and see what suits you best.

COSMO FLOSS

Cosmo floss is also a six-strand embroidery floss and can be found in more than 440 colors. There are currently three types of Cosmo floss: cotton floss, seasons (a variegated floss), and Nishikiito (a metallic thread).

Cosmo is slightly pricier than DMC floss. It runs a little more than $1 per skein. If you want to upgrade for a special project, you'll feel like you are treating yourself. Many stores carry the entire range of colors.

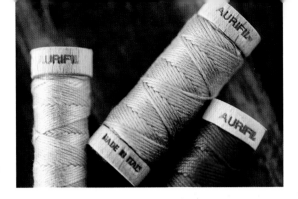

The first difference that you will notice when you handle Cosmo floss is how smooth the thread is, noticeably different from DMC floss. It is not a satin floss, but has the feel of satin, which means it is a dream to work with. I rarely have tangles when I am stitching with Cosmo's cotton floss.

Speaking of dreamy, the Nishikiito thread is a must try! This thread is made using techniques for Japanese Gold Thread. I have never held authentic gold thread, but I can imagine how precious it must feel. It was traditionally made by taking real gold and pounding it until it became thin enough to adhere a layer onto paper. It was then cut into tiny strips and carefully wound around a core of silk thread. This is an extremely simplified version of a delicate process, but the end result was a thread that truly shone. Those of you familiar with metallic thread, know the challenges of stitching with it: tangles that don't want to untangle, knots that don't want to unknot and thread that does the opposite of anything you want it to do! If you love the look of sparkle in your stitching, but the thought of using metallic thread makes you want to run in the other direction, give this thread a try. Just dive right in and start collecting colors, because once you try it, you will be hooked. It threads through the needle easily, rarely tangles, and looks gorgeous in your embroidery. This is a single strand thread and does not need to be divided. I use two strands together (one long thread, folded in half and knotted at the end) because, again, I like to see my stitches.

AURIFLOSS WOODEN SPOOLS

Need I say anything else? This cotton floss comes on adorable wooden spools, neatly packaged up in boxes of ten colors. No matter how gently I handle my skeins, I end up with jumbles of colored thread. I have never been one for winding them onto little cards, so I end up with tangles, but I never have a jumbled mess of colors with these little spools.

Aurifloss comes in 270 colors and is pricier than both DMC and Cosmo. A spool of 18 yards will cost you $4–$6. Your best value is to purchase a box of ten colors, usually curated by a designer and matching a fabric line. While I like to choose my own colors, designer hand-picked colors from a collection (on wooden spools!) really appeal to me. This is a six-strand cotton floss like DMC and Cosmo.

When you open your small white box, you will notice that the colors do not have the shiny look that Cosmo floss has. There is a rustic feel to these threads, as if they would be right at home stitched onto a sampler of linen fabric. If you are working on a project where you want your threads to shine, you might choose Cosmo over Aurifloss. If you want your project to have more of a matte organic look, Aurifloss would be your choice.

Although I have not noticed much tangling while stitching with Aurifloss, if I am using all six strands together, they do not thread through a needle as easily as DMC or Cosmo floss does. This is easily remedied by running the end of the floss through Thread Heaven or beeswax before threading.

ELEGANZA PERLE COTTON

If you follow along with my stitching on Instagram, then you know how much I love Eleganza threads! These threads are a collaboration between Sue Spargo and WonderFil Specialty Threads. There are ninety colors available, and if you love color, these are the threads for you. The color palette is saturated with such irresistible options as Sea Glass, Sari, Lagoon, and Fuchsia Fever.

The price of Eleganza is a bargain at just $4–$6 per spool. Each spool has 40–70 yards of thread. I use this thread in most of my projects, and I have not run out of a color yet!

These are not six-strand threads like DMC, Cosmo, and Aurifloss, but rather a single strand of perle cotton. The perle cotton brings a delightful spiraled texture to each stitch, making your finished embroidery appear more delicate and detailed.

This thread comes in three weights: size 8, size 5, and size 3. Size 8 is comparable to four strands of cotton floss, and size 5 is comparable to six strands of cotton floss. Size 3 is the thickest and comparable to eight strands of cotton floss.

If you like the look of variegated floss, then you need to try the variegated colors of Eleganza perle cotton. With DMC variegated floss, you will see a change of color about every 4", while Cosmo changes color about every 3"–11". The variegation pattern of Eleganza is extra short, which means you will see the change of color more often. I sometimes find myself impatient with DMC color variations because I want to see the colors shift and shimmer more with greater frequency.

If you like the color palette available in Eleganza threads, but want a thread with more sparkle or shine, then you need to try Razzle and Dazzle, also offered by Sue Spargo and WonderFil Specialty Threads. These threads are both size 8 weight, much like the weight of a perle cotton. I do not have problems with these threads slipping out of the needle or tangling, like some satin threads are known to do. Razzle is made of 100% rayon and is much like a satin thread from the other brands. Dazzle is also made of 100% rayon but it has a metallic strand running through it, which gives it sparkle. It is not as sparkly as the Cosmo Nishikiito, so if you want something fancy but not over the top, try the Dazzle.

let's talk needles

You might walk into the craft store and think "a needle is a needle" and you plan on buying the first pack you see. Until you actually look at the wall of needles and are overwhelmed with all the brands and types. Let's demystify that process.

Needles are numbered, which indicates the fine-ness. The smaller the number, the larger the needle will be. For example, a size 3 needle will be thicker than a size 7 needle. Embroidery needles are commonly sized from 1 to 12, with size 1 being the largest and 12 the smallest. My favorite size needles are 7 and 9, but yours may be something completely different. If you are brand new to embroidery, I suggest buying a variety pack of needles so that you can experiment with several types and sizes before you decide on your favorite. If you are not brand new, pick your favorite trusty needle and you are ready to go!

I use hand appliqué needles, sometimes called Sharps or even Milliner's Needles, for many of these projects because the needle will be going through several layers of fabric, and a very sharp needle does not fray the fabric. You will notice that as your needle becomes dull from use, it will not sharply pierce the fabric. Instead it will fray the fabric, and your stitches will not look as smooth as they could with a fresh needle. Throw away those bent and dull needles because you will just end up becoming aggravated when you have to spend time trimming tiny frayed fabric bits. (I am most definitely speaking from experience, and I want to save you from yourself: replace your needles!)

You will find that just as there are varying price points with thread, the same is true of needles. Clover, Dritz, and Fons & Porter are brands that your local fabric and craft store will most likely carry. Tulip Hiroshima needles come packaged in miniature glass vials and sell for $8–$10 a pack. There is a definite smoothness that you will notice when you stitch with a Tulip needle, but in my opinion a less expensive needle will work just as well as the more expensive brands. Every once in a while, I succumb to the draw of a more expensive needle, because how can you resist a tiny glass vial full of needles?

If you have not bought hand-sewing needles before and want to try an assortment of several types and sizes to find a favorite, Dritz makes small round cases filled with various needle sizes. It is a great way to buy several types of needle to experiment with until you find which works best for you.

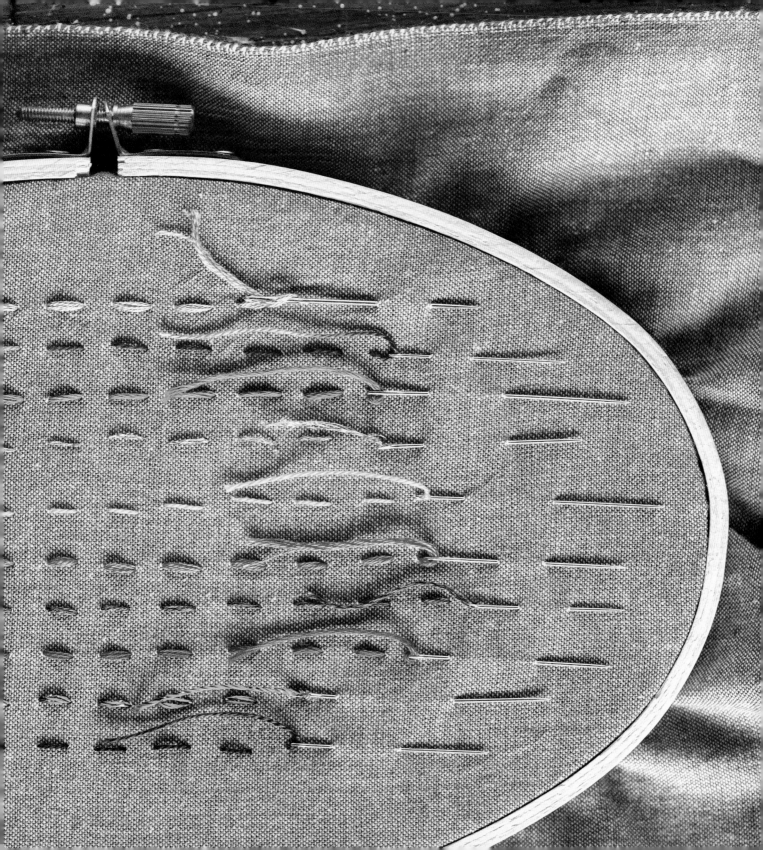

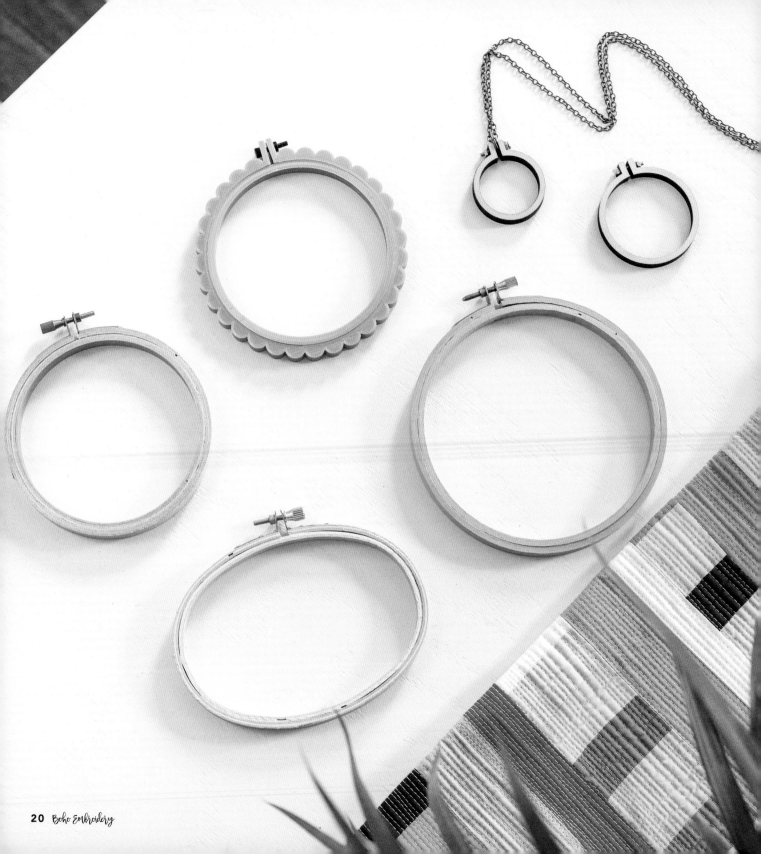

let's talk hoops

An embroidery hoop has a dual purpose: It holds your fabric taut, making it easier to embroider, and it displays your finished project, acting as a frame. There are some fun variations available.

WOODEN HOOPS

A simple wooden hoop is inexpensive and can be found at any craft or fabric store. If you are fortunate to have thrift or secondhand stores nearby, check these out for vintage hoops. Like most items built in the past, antique hoops can be much sturdier than the hoops you will find in your local craft store today. Snatch them up if you find them! Or, leave them there and text me, and I'll be by to add them to my stash!

3-D PRINTED HOOPS

If you want to take your work up to the next level, you will be as excited as I was when I first discovered 3-D printed hoops. Who knew you could print a hoop? My favorite is made by Julia Eigenbrodt of Stars & Sunshine. She and her husband built a 3D printer for an anniversary project and ever since, she has been printing whimsical hoops in a rainbow of colors, like gold and translucent blue and green. Each hoop is designed and printed by her on her 3D printer and then assembled with hardware before reaching you. Forget the pastel-colored plastic hoops of the past; this is a new breed of hoop,

sophisticated and chic! These can be purchased online through Julia's Etsy shop (see Resources, page 114).

MINI-HOOPS

You may love the look of hoop art but aren't sure how to display it around your house. With mini wooden hoops created by Sonia Lyne of Dandelyne, you can create a piece of hoop art that is small enough to wear around your neck. Sonia may just be the most bursting-with-positivity, creative person that you will meet in the online world! The hoops are hand-crafted in Australia and can be purchased online in Dandeylne's Etsy shop (see Resources, page 114).

let's talk scissors

Some tools are per personal preference, so please choose whatever floss, needles, or hoops that suit your fancy. You can ignore all of my suggestions and use a favorite brand you have found on your own. However, you will want these exact scissors before starting on any of the projects in this book: Fiskars Micro-Tip scissors. Fiskars makes them in both the swing and the spring-action versions. The swing version works just fine for general cutting, but the spring-action version is perfect for fussy cutting tiny and precise areas. The spring action allows the scissors (and not your hands!) to do the cutting work.

I also recommend stashing a few small pair of ordinary embroidery scissors wherever you plan on doing your embroidery. Keep one in your workbox, one on your desk, one with your floss. You can never have too many scissors!

let's talk marking tools

There will be times when you want to draw grid lines or make small marks on your embroidery project to trace the path of a line of stitches. There are three types of marking tools that I use, and all three make marks that will be removed from the fabric when you have finished stitching.

note:: *Even though I have had great success with the products I am including, always test, test, test. Especially before you trace a pattern onto your great-grandmother's ancient linens!*

HEAT ERASABLE: CLOVER WHITE MARKING PEN

This marking pen really does erase completely away with heat. Write on your fabric, stitch over the markings, and then when you are done stitching and want the white markings to completely disappear, gently press the iron over your fabric. The marks will be gone!

HEAT ERASABLE: PILOT FRIXION ERASABLE PENS

When you need to see your lines clearly, these FriXion pens do a good job. They erase with heat like the Clover products, which means that you can place your finished project on an ironing board and gently press the iron across your marks and they will disappear. One thing to note: If your stitches do not completely cover the pen lines, there is a chance that you will see a faint trace of the line you drew. Choose a pen color that is light enough to see, but is not so dark that it will leave marks on your fabric.

WATER-SOLUBLE: CHALK

My favorite way to mark on fabric is using chalk. Chalk lines can easily be brushed away or washed out with water. Because chalk is available in a variety of widths, test it on a piece of scrap fabric before you use it on your actual project to make sure it's what you want. One thing to note: Because chalk is intended to brush off easily, the chalk lines may brush away prematurely if you are carrying the project around with you.

A fairly inexpensive brand of chalk pencil that I like is Dritz quilting chalk, which can be found in the sewing notions section of your favorite fabric stores. This chalk is thin and comes with a holder so that it feels like you are working with a pencil.

WATER-SOLUBLE: PENCILS

If you like the ease of working with chalk but want a thinner writing instrument, the Clover water-soluble pencils will be your go-to tool. Available in your local fabric store, they are

sold in a pack of three colors: white, pink and blue. They write extremely smoothly and leave a strong visible line. I also like that these pencils come with caps. I like to keep one in my ArtBin with whatever project I am currently working on, and because of the cap I do not have to worry about these pencils accidentally marking up my fabric.

A slightly more expensive version of the Clover pencil is the Karisma mechanical pencil, which is Japanese made and can be found online. I have a weakness for embroidery notions that are made in Japan, and this pencil is no exception! The Karisma mechanical pencil will give you a thinner pencil line, and if you like the ease of working with chalk, this feels less clumsy to work with than a chalk holder, because it is an actual mechanical pencil. You can use water to erase these pencil lines, or a Little House fabric eraser which also works well with these pencils.

WATER-SOLUBLE: PENS

There are two kinds of water-soluble pen I like to use and both are made by Dritz: the Mark-B-Gone marking pen and the quilting, fine point Mark-B-Gone pen. Both pens write in blue.

let's talk adhesives

FUSIBLE INTERFACING

I buy HeatnBond Lite by the 25-yard bolt, and it is my number one choice for preparing appliqué for embroidery. When you look at this interfacing, you will see a shiny side and a dull, paper-backed side. The shiny side is ironed to the wrong side of the fabric, and once it cools, the paper is peeled off. From there, you can fuse your appliqué to another piece of fabric so it stays in place while you embroider. HeatnBond can be found by the bolt at fabric stores and in smaller packages at craft stores.

WHITE ALL-PURPOSE GLUE

Your bottle of white glue is not just for elementary school projects anymore! This glue works great on fabric. I use this when I am finished stitching a hoop and want to permanently secure the fabric onto the hoop (see page 64).

GLUE STICK

Glue sticks are floating around everywhere at my house. I like them because the glue is washable and it is a secure bond that is also removable. I will sometimes use a glue stick to secure a small appliqué to a bigger piece before I stitch over it. It holds the fabric in place, dries nicely, and can be stitched over without gumming up my needle or distorting the fabric.

let's talk paint and stain

Painting or staining your wood hoop is a way to take your hoop art to the next level: not just a piece of embroidery in a hoop, but a work of art in a frame.

I like to use acrylic paint and a small angled-tip brush for painting my hoops. I have a variety of widths of brush, but the important thing is the 45 degree angle. This angled tip on the brush allows you to reach small spaces near the hoop hardware. Pick your favorite brand of paint and keep a few bottles of your favorite colors on hand. Try painting the hoop all one color and then add accent stripes in another. Follow the directions on the bottle for drying times. Do not put your fabric into a hoop that is still wet with paint.

Staining a hoop is another option, especially if you plan to hang your hoop on a gallery wall and want it to coordinate with frames that you already have. I like how stain adds a rustic feel to your hoop art. It is incredibly easy, and you could probably stain hoops for the rest of your life with one small can of stain. I like to use a cotton swab or even a folded up paper towel as my "brush" for stain, because it allows for thorough coverage on the sides of the hoop. Follow the manufacturer's directions for use and drying times.

Natural

Espresso

Ebony

Honey

Grey

Oak

Driftwood

Pine

Chestnut

MINWAX®
COLOR GUIDE
GUÍA DE COLORES

let's talk extras!

There are a few tools worth having that will make creating some of this book's projects much easier. You don't need to have all these tools to start, but it will help to read this list over before you decide which project to do first.

LIGHTBOX

Using a small lightbox will make tracing the patterns from this book easier. By placing your image on the lightbox and then tracing onto freezer paper or HeatnBond, you can easily transfer images to prepare them for embroidery. In a pinch, if you do not have access to a lightbox, an alternative is to use a window.

When I am transferring a large image that does not fit on my lightbox, I tape the pattern to the window and place my freezer paper or HeatnBond on top of that. It is also helpful to have a lightbox when you are working at night and do not have the light from a window to use.

FREEZER PAPER

Freezer paper works well if you want to transfer an image to fabric. You trace the image on the dull side of the freezer paper and then iron it to the fabric, shiny-side down. The freezer paper is removable and can even be reused. So if you need a dozen hexie shapes for a project, you can draw one hexie on a piece of freezer paper and then reuse it for all twelve fabric hexies.

Freezer paper can be purchased at the grocery store in the baking aisle; I have never found it at a craft store, even though I suspect crafters are probably the primary buyers of freezer paper these days.

COLORED PENCILS AND MARKERS

Did you know that you can add colored details to fabric with pencils and markers? It's true! Have a selection of colored pencils or thin markers at the ready for adding small bits of color to your project. You can mark the fabric with a watercolor pencil and then diffuse the color throughout the fabric using a small damp paintbrush.

Markers also work great for adding very small details of color rather than using stitches. I like to use colored pencils for eye and hair detail. This probably goes without saying, but do not wash your project after you have added marker or pencil detail. The colors may bleed, or disappear entirely, in water. Always test your marker and pencil on scrap fabric before you use them in your project.

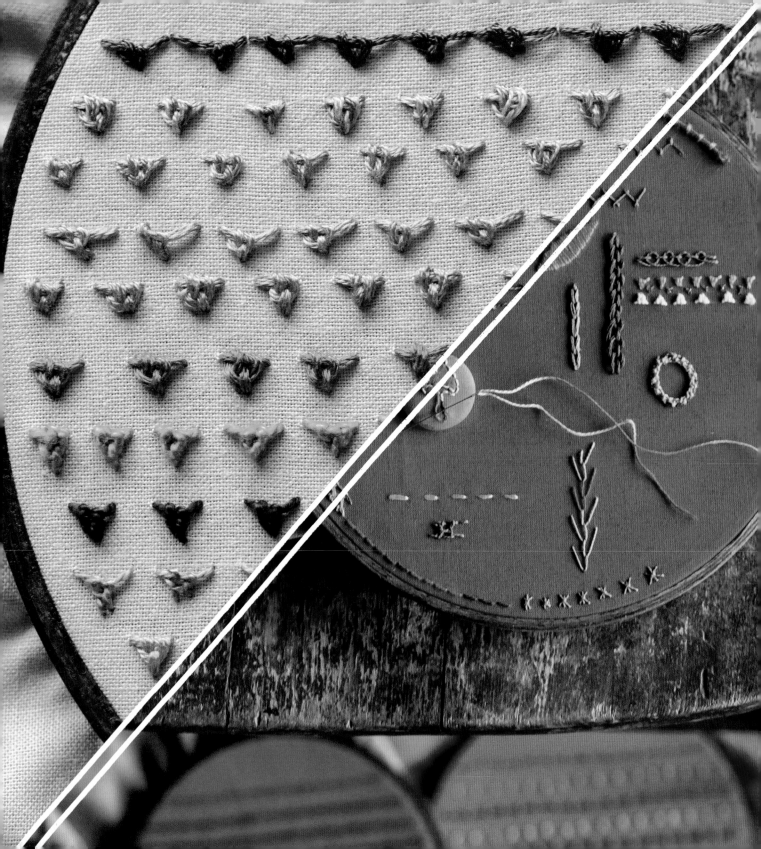

CHAPTER 2

Let's Talk About

MY FAVORITE
STITCHES

THE STITCH SAMPLER

A Cross Stitch B Couching Stitch

C Chain Stitch D Straight Stitch

E Coral Stitch F Herringbone Stitch

G Pekinese Stitch H Backstitch

I Satin Stitch J Stem Stitch

K Running Stitch L Trellis Spiral Stitch

M Sheaf Stitch N Feather Stitch

O Fishbone Stitch P Danish Knot

the stitch dictionary

The stitches in this chapter are the most common ones that I use. There are an endless variety of stitches in the embroidery world, but I have hand-picked this selection for you because they will work well with all the projects in this book, and I am confident that they will inspire you to create your own combinations.

I included some alternatives to popular stitches. For instance, the Danish knot rather than the French knot. The Danish knot can stand alone on fabrics with busy designs. Bold stitches such as this help you to highlight and enhance aspects of the fabric that you chose. You can easily use another resource to learn a French knot (see Resources, page 114), but how often do you hear about the Danish knot? Exactly!

I have divided the stitches into two categories: primary and secondary. For every primary stitch, a loosely based secondary stitch will follow. I have also given suggestions on how you can use each stitch as you create your own hoop art.

This is by no means an exhaustive lesson on stitches. If you are looking to add an even greater number of hand stitches to your repertoire, the two books that I like to keep by my side in my workroom for reference are *The Embroidery Stitch Bible* by Betty Barnden and *Embroidery Stitches: Over 400 Contemporary and Traditional Stitch Patterns* by Mary Webb.

The Resources section (see page 114) also includes suggestions for helpful video tutorials and other inspirational sources for stitches.

Sometimes, to break out of a creative rut, I like to make myself learn a new stitch and then create a project based on that. Try this if you are feeling like your creativity is waning.

PRACTICE HOOP

I recommend that you keep a practice hoop alongside whatever project you are working on. Choose a fabric that you like looking at, because it will be in your workspace, and place it in a medium-size hoop.

Having a practice hoop in progress all the time, allows you to experiment with stitches and threads without feeling like you are beginning a new project. There is the bonus of having somewhere convenient to stash your threaded needles, which lets you stop and start easily. And, when you have run out of room on your practice hoop, you have something pretty to display in your workspace. Be proud of your stitches!

STRAIGHT STITCH (primary)

>> **GREAT FOR:** detail, texture

Thread your needle and quickly get stitching with this stitch. It does not matter in which direction you work — just place the stitches where you want them to be. Start with your needle under your fabric. Position needle and pull thread up through the fabric at A. Decide the length of your stitch and pull your needle through to the underneath of the fabric at B.

try this! *Create a wrapped rose, which is several straight stitches varied diagonally to create a geometric floral design. Begin with a sideways square of straight stitches. Stitch four stitches in a square around the sideways square. Keep adding four stitches, varying how they are placed. You will soon see a flower appear. Keep adding stitches until the flower is to your liking.*

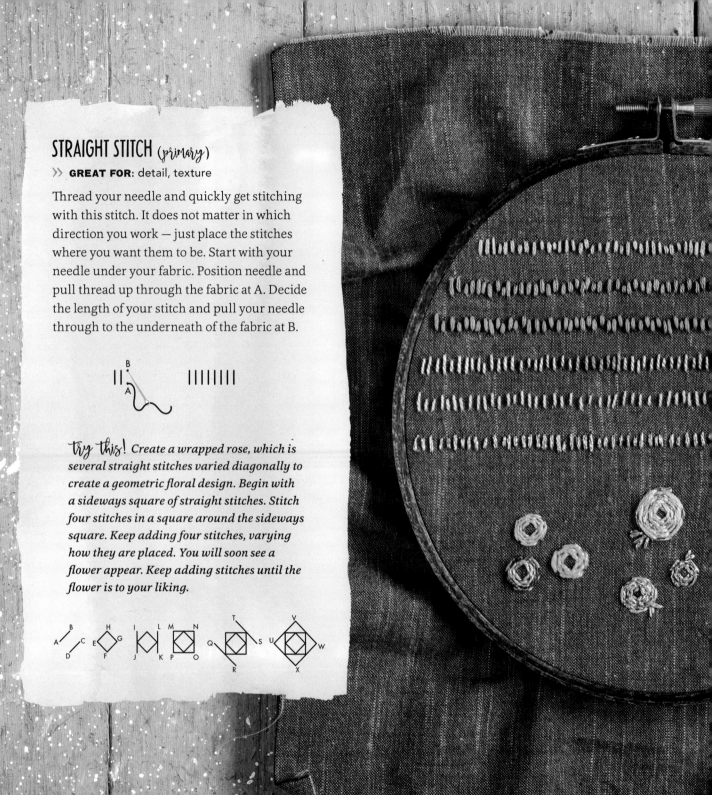

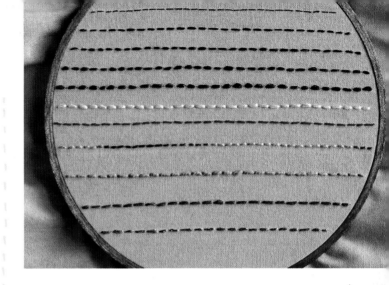

SATIN STITCH (*secondary*)

>> **GREAT FOR:** filling stitch, decorative

Satin stitching is used to fill an area, such as a petal on a flower or a geometric shape. Tip: For bigger areas, I find it helpful to place several stitches throughout your shape to use as guides. From there, you can continue to fill in the gaps with satin stitching. This technique helps you to keep your stitches even throughout the shape you are filling in.

Bring needle up at A and down at B. Continue until your shape is filled.

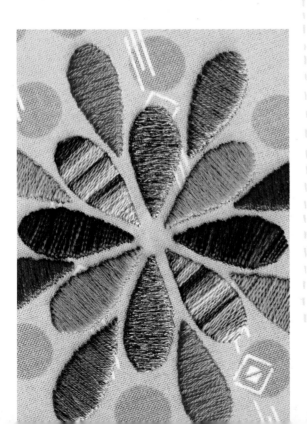

BACKSTITCH (*primary*)

>> **GREAT FOR:** borders

The backstitch is a simple stitch that looks great as a border around the outside of your hoop, and it has just as much impact when you use it to highlight areas of fabric. Notice in the sampler that one or two strands of thread will make a delicate line, while four to six strands of thread will make a bolder statement.

Bring needle up at A and down at B. Continue until you want your line to end.

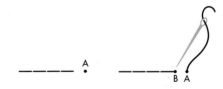

try this! *Play with numbers! 1) Use a combination of two-strand and four-strand stitches throughout your project. 2) Work a circular border with six strands of thread around the inside of your hoop and then stitch a three-strand border parallel to that.*

SHEAF STITCH (Secondary)

>> **GREAT FOR:** decorative, straight lines

The sheaf stitch is a decorative stitch that can be scattered throughout your work. If you have the patience, it can also be a bold choice as a circular border around your project. It is a great stitch for hand embroidering over a seam in the fabric.

try this! *1) Make your sheaf with five stitches instead of three. 2) Use a different thread color for the stitch that wraps around the middle. 3) Make the middle stitch slightly longer than the two end stitches.*

Start with three backstitches next to each other. Pull needle up through the fabric at A and pass under the stitches towards the left. Pass the needle under all three stitches from the right (without going under the fabric). Bring the needle down through the fabric close to point A to cinch and secure the stitch.

RUNNING STITCH (primary)

>> **GREAT FOR:** straight lines

It doesn't get any more basic than the running stitch, and yet if you look at Sashiko designs, they look anything but basic. Sashiko, which means "little stabs," is a traditional form of Japanese embroidery that uses repeated running stitches to create patterns. Master this stitch and you are on your way to learning an entirely new form of embroidery. Or just master this stitch so that you can add nice straight stitches to your project. This stitch can be varied in length for a different look.

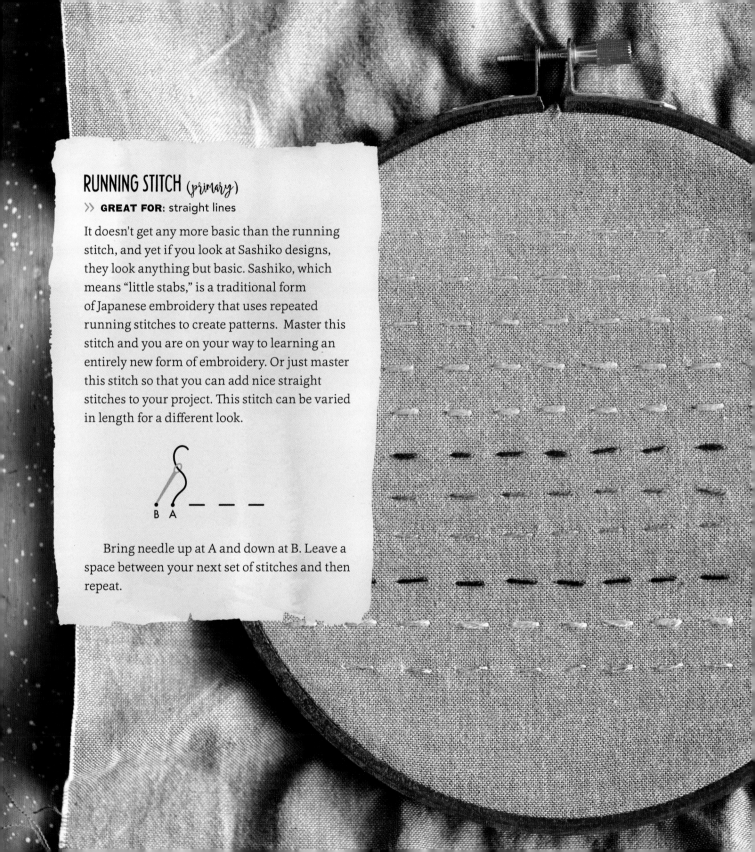

Bring needle up at A and down at B. Leave a space between your next set of stitches and then repeat.

COUCHING STITCH *(Secondary)*

>> **GREAT FOR:** straight and curved lines

Couching is another simple stitch than can give your work visual impact. You can drastically change the appearance of this stitch by using the same color thread for both the horizontal (foundation) stitches and vertical stitches or by using two or more colors.

try this! *For a thick strand of couching, cut apart several colorful hair elastics and use these as your base thread. This will give a dramatic raised effect. Place the hair elastic on the fabric where you want to start stitching and begin your attaching stitches.*

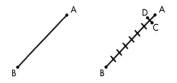

Bring the needle with your foundation thread up at A and down at B. This may be a long thread since B will be the point where you want your row of stitching to end. This can be a straight or curved line. (Alternative: Bring your needle up at A and keep your thread above the fabric so that you can move it where you want it while you are attaching your stitches.) Bring the needle with the new thread up at C and down at D. You are making the stitches that hold your foundation thread in place. These stitches can be spaced as far apart as you would like them.

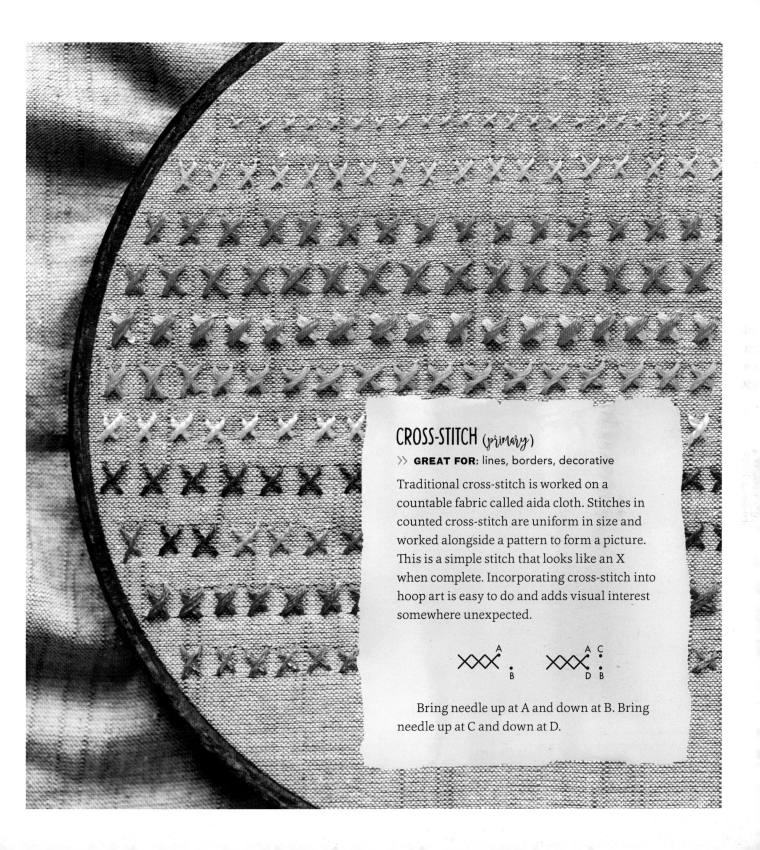

CROSS-STITCH (primary)

>> **GREAT FOR:** lines, borders, decorative

Traditional cross-stitch is worked on a countable fabric called aida cloth. Stitches in counted cross-stitch are uniform in size and worked alongside a pattern to form a picture. This is a simple stitch that looks like an X when complete. Incorporating cross-stitch into hoop art is easy to do and adds visual interest somewhere unexpected.

Bring needle up at A and down at B. Bring needle up at C and down at D.

HERRINGBONE STITCH (*Secondary*)

>> **GREAT FOR:** borders, lines

The herringbone stitch is good for hand stitching near or over fabric seams. The sampler shows three versions of this stitch: basic herringbone (Rows 1, 2 and 8), tied herringbone (Rows 3, 4, 5 and 9), and herringbone ladder (Rows 6, 7 and 10). There are even more variations on this stitch — check the reference books I mentioned previously for several other suggestions.

> *Tip: I like to avoid unnecessary steps whenever possible, but to get precise lines on the herringbone, it is best to draw a top and bottom set of parallel lines to guide your stitches. Use chalk, a water-soluble pen or a heat-erasable pen and a ruler.*

Basic Herringbone Stitch

Bring needle up at A. At B, bring needle tip down and then up at C and pull thread through. Bring needle tip down at D and up at E and pull thread through. Continue and finish by pulling thread below fabric.

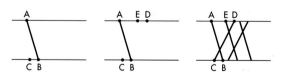

Tied Herringbone Stitch

Work a row of herringbone stitches and then work a small backstitch over the X in each stitch.

Herringbone Ladder Stitch

Work two rows of backstitches. Make sure one row is slightly offset. Bring needle up at A and slide needle under the stitch by A, going over your working thread. Pull through. Take needle to the stitch below and repeat. Continue at stitch C, then D, and repeat until you reach the end of your backstitch rows.

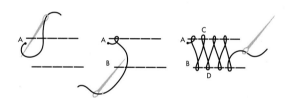

> *Tip: For the herringbone ladder stitch, I find it easiest to keep rotating the hoop as I work–first a top stitch then a bottom stitch, so that it looks like I am stitching the rungs of a ladder.*

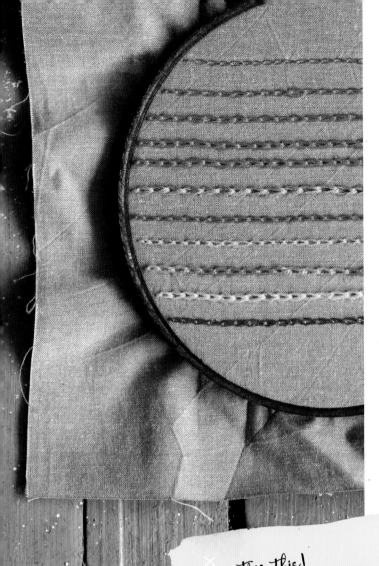

CHAIN STITCH (primary)

>> **GREAT FOR:** curved and straight lines, borders, outlines

I love the braided appearance of the chain stitch. I relearned this stitch ages ago via instructions from Jenny Hart of *Sublime Stitching*. It completely changed how I felt about the chain stitch.

Make a small backstitch from A to B. Bring needle up at C and slip it under the backstitch. Take needle down as close to C as possible. Continue this stitch by going under both threads of each previous chain stitch as you progress.

try this!

1) To make a "lazy daisy," create individual chain stitches beginning with a small backstitch and working in the shape of a circle so that you end up with a flower shape. 2) Scatter individual chain stitches for texture in a project.

FEATHER STITCH (*Secondary*)

>> **GREAT FOR:** lines, decorative

The feather stitch is considered an open chain stitch, and as you work it, you will understand why. Work this stitch from the top to the bottom. This stitch would be perfect to use as leaves or vines on a project.

> *tip: You will always bring your needle up through the fabric on the center line and down through the fabric on either side.*

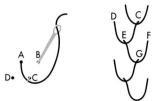

Bring the needle up at A and down at B. Before pulling the thread all the way through at B, bring the needle back up at C to form a 'U'. Then down at D but before pulling the thread all the way through, back up at E. Repeat until you achieve the desired chain length.

> *try this! 1) On your practice hoop, experiment with short and long anchor stitches. Watch how it transforms the shape of your feather stitch. 2) For textural interest, try matching the thread color to the fabric you are stitching on.*

CORAL STITCH *(primary)*

>> **GREAT FOR:** lines, borders

I love how the coral stitch looks like a stretched-out handwritten font, full of loops. This has a carefree feel to it and is a great stitch to use for hair or to show wind. Have fun and play around with this one! I find it easiest to work this stitch from bottom to top, which means you will be holding your work sideways.

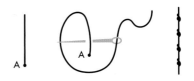

Pull needle up through the fabric at A. Place your thread on your fabric in a straight line. Make an upside-down U with the thread and hold it in place as you put your needle where you want your next stitch to be. Make a small stitch with the needle. Pull the needle through. Repeat until you achieve the desired length.

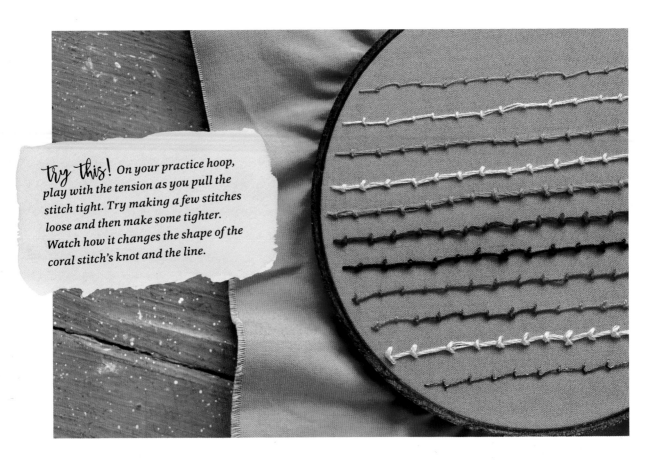

try this! On your practice hoop, play with the tension as you pull the stitch tight. Try making a few stitches loose and then make some tighter. Watch how it changes the shape of the coral stitch's knot and the line.

DANISH KNOT (Secondary)

>> **GREAT FOR:** decorative, texture, detail

Because the projects in this book use detailed fabrics, I like to use a knot that looks substantial. I predict that the Danish knot will soon be your go-to knot for detail stitches or for filling entire areas with texture.

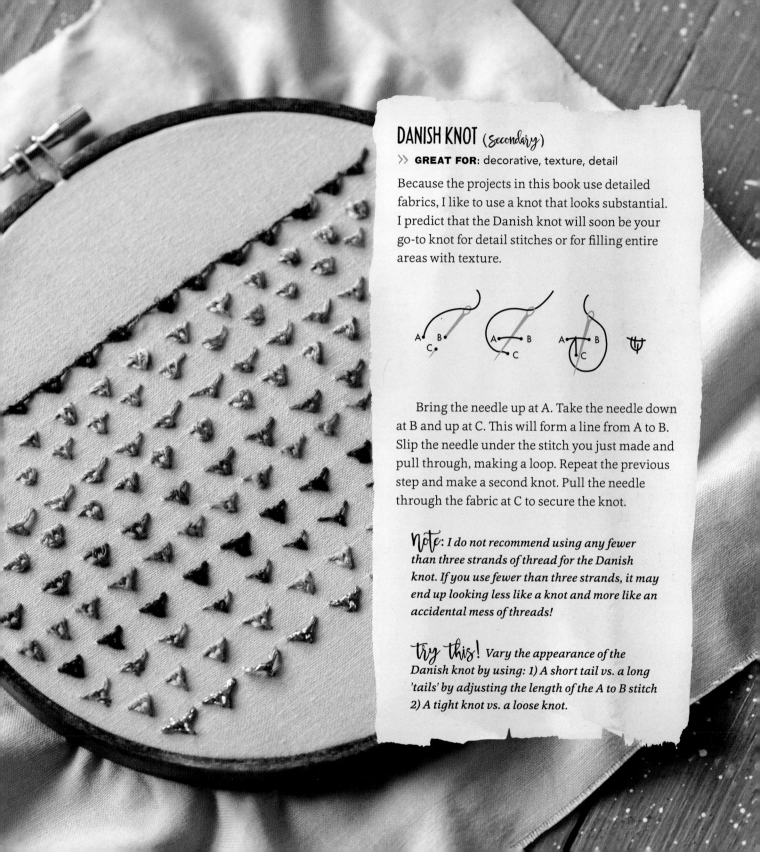

Bring the needle up at A. Take the needle down at B and up at C. This will form a line from A to B. Slip the needle under the stitch you just made and pull through, making a loop. Repeat the previous step and make a second knot. Pull the needle through the fabric at C to secure the knot.

Note: *I do not recommend using any fewer than three strands of thread for the Danish knot. If you use fewer than three strands, it may end up looking less like a knot and more like an accidental mess of threads!*

try this! *Vary the appearance of the Danish knot by using: 1) A short tail vs. a long 'tails' by adjusting the length of the A to B stitch 2) A tight knot vs. a loose knot.*

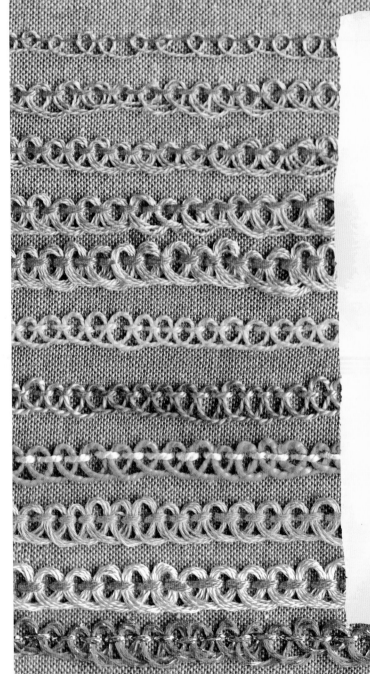

PEKINESE STITCH (primary)

>> **GREAT FOR:** lines, borders, decorative

The Pekinese stitch is a lovely, lace-like stitch. This stitch is worked from left to right and is built on a base of backstitches.

Begin with a row of backstitches. Bring the needle up at A, close to the first backstitch. Stitching above the fabric, take your thread under the second backstitch (B) and then under the previous backstitch (C) while going over your thread. Still stitching above the fabric, continue until you reach the end of your backstitch row and bring the working thread through to the back of the fabric.

Hint: *You will always be going forward two backstitches and back one backstitch while you are weaving the Pekinese stitch.*

try this! *1) Use a variegated thread for a colorful look with minimum thread changes. 2) Use a solid color for the backstitch and a metallic thread for the stitch that gets woven through the backstitch.*

TRELLIS SPIRAL STITCH (*Secondary*)

>> **GREAT FOR:** decorative, circles

Like the Pekinese stitch, the trellis stitch is stitched onto a backstitch foundation and then woven above the fabric. Once you feel comfortable with this stitch, if you're like me, you will want to add this decorative stitch to anything floral.

Begin with a row of backstitches in the final shape you want to stitch. Bring needle up at A. Work in a counter-clockwise direction (though if you are left-handed, it will be easier for you to work in a clockwise direction) around your backstitch foundation. Take needle under the next backstitch and over your working thread. Pull through loosely creating a nice loop. This may take some practice to get the tension right. Continue until you reach point A where you began. Work the next row in exactly the same way by using your previous stitches to continue the weaving. When you are finished stitching, pull the needle through the fabric underneath the final stitch.

STEM STITCH (primary)

>> **GREAT FOR:** curves, borders, texture

I really like how this stitch easily achieves a slightly twisted appearance, making it a perfect choice when you want a straight line of stitching that is less severe than a running stitch or a backstitch.

Bring needle up at A and down at B, making a diagonal line. Bring needle up at C (about the middle of your first stitch) and down at D. Continue for your chosen length.

FISHBONE STITCH (Secondary)

>> **GREAT FOR:** filling stitch

This stitch is perfect for filling in a teardrop or circular shape or use it by itself to create a feather or tree shape. It can be helpful to draw a center line down the length of your shape and be sure that each diagonal stitch is slightly over that drawn line to create the fishbone effect.

try this! Work the stitches farther apart or closer together while keeping to the shape to see how the appearance changes.

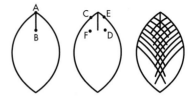

Make a straight stitch from A to B (along the center line if you marked one). Your next diagonal straight stitches will cross over the first stitch line. Bring needle up at C, down at D slightly to the right of the A/B stitch, then up at E and down at F slightly to the left of the A/B stitch. Continue forming your stitches each stitch crossing over the previous one and watch as the fishbone shape appears.

CHAPTER 3

✕ ✕ ✕ ✕ ✕ ✕ ✕ ✕ ✕ ✕ ✕

Let's Talk About

FABRIC

working with color

Aside from minimal time spent learning basic color wheel skills in my high school art classes, I have not been professionally trained to wield a color wheel and cite color rules that you must apply to your art. I do, however, know what I like when it comes to choosing colors for a project. In fact, it is one of my favorite parts of the creative process. When I feel like I am hitting a brick wall and creativity has temporarily left me, I just need to play around with color. I cut up some squares of fabric, add in a few skeins of thread, and ideas once again start to flow.

We each have colors that we gravitate toward. What are the go-to colors you choose when decorating a room in your house, or that show up in your favorite outfits? These are the colors that make you feel comfortable. Your palette might be beach-inspired subdued ivory, blue, and yellow — or it could be bursting with jeweled-toned purple, green, orange, and navy. Identify your color palette and the remaining decisions will seem simple from there.

My favorite color palette is featured in this hoop made with Sarah Watson's Garden Secrets fabric: greens, golds, mustard, coral, and teal. It is a palette I never tire of, and I include it in everything from decorating to clothing to the hoops I make.

Fabric and threads can be powerful creative influences on color selection. Sometimes it is as easy as stopping by the craft store for a bundle of colorful threads and then choosing fabric based on that. And then, of course, there are fabrics that grab your attention and you know you have to make something with them, even if you aren't sure just what yet. Which colors will you emphasize and embellish with your stitches?

Once you have decided on your palette, the next step is deciding what type of fabric you are going to choose for your first project.

selecting fabric types

What I like most about working with fabric as the palette for my art, is how versatile it can be. Whatever your price range, you do not need to spend a lot of money to begin creating. Your supplies do not need to take up much space. A few fabric basics can get you started while you decide which materials you like to work with. If you are familiar with the wonderful world of fabric obsession, then you probably have everything that you need already in your sewing space. But I'm not going to sit here and tell you not to buy any more fabric before starting on a project, because most likely you have an online shopping basket full of

½ yard cuts of fabric that you are just looking for an excuse to buy. Let a new hoop art project be your excuse!

Just as a painter would use more than one type or color of paint to achieve a textured effect, you will be doing the same thing with your fabric. Learning how to blend various types of fabric together to achieve your desired look will be a trial and error process. I have scrapped complete hoops because the fabrics that I pictured in my head didn't look right once I tried to blend them together. The wool that I tried to mix with the more delicate batik didn't look artfully layered but instead just

seemed haphazard in its placement. Don't be afraid to scrap something that just doesn't seem to be working. If you don't love it as you are putting it together, you will not love it anymore as you spend hours staring at it while you stitch. Fortunately, you are not constructing a garment, which requires precise measurements and larger quantities of fabric. Hoop art only requires small quantities of fabric, which gives you the freedom to play around with bits of fabric without feeling wasteful if you decide not to use them. When purchasing fabric, depending on the size of your hoop or canvas, you can purchase several fat quarters and this will provide you with more than enough fabric for a project. It may even leave you extra to start something new.

So let's talk about the types of fabric you will see whether you are doing your shopping online or in a fabric store.

QUILTING COTTON

Quilting cotton is my first choice when selecting fabrics to make a hoop. It is sturdy and holds up well to stitching. The color and pattern choices far surpass that of other types of fabric, and new collections are released several times a year.

I do not wash my fabric before using it for hoops so that the fabric remains crisp, which makes it easier to stitch on.

Always check the scale of the patterns on the fabric before making your final choice. If you are at a brick and mortar store and can see the fabric for yourself, this is not generally an issue. But, if you are like me and live far from a

quilting shop, then you are doing most of your fabric shopping online. My favorite online fabric stores (see Resources, page 114) are the ones that tell you the measurements of the largest pattern on the fabric. I check this before purchasing anything so that I'm not surprised when I open a fabric package.

CHAMBRAY

Chambray is a sturdy fabric, like quilting cotton, yet it feels lighter and has a bit of a drape to it. I like the multicolored look of the chambray weave. This weave is the result of having a colored thread as the warp (the lengthwise threads), then weaving a white thread as the weft (the cross-wse threads), over and under the warp. Chambray makes an excellent textured background, but it also works well for detailed appliqués in your hoop art.

LINEN

Linen is made from the fibers of the flax plant. It is a lightweight fabric popular for summer garments (if you don't mind the wrinkles). I love the natural look it lends to hoop art. Some linens are more textured than others, depending upon how much processing the flax has undergone. Pair linen with a stained hoop and you are on your way to a rustic-looking finished product. Linen is widely available in both solid colors and patterned designs. It is easy to stitch on, but because it has a drapey hand and can continue to stretch even when tightened in a hoop, I recommend you choose a tighter weave.

KNIT

When you think of knit fabric, you most likely think of a flowy shirt or a cozy pair of pajamas that you wear around the house. But did you know that knit is not just for garments? Jersey knit can be made from natural cotton and wool or from synthetic fibers. Because it is a fabric with a lot of drape, it will not make a good background to base your hoop on. But knit fabric appliqués can be easily stitched through and curl nicely around the raw edges, making it a great fabric to use for adding details and dimension. Knit fabrics can be found in an array of solid colors and patterns.

DENIM

Denim has a lovely textured appearance and is woven much like chambray. The white thread in the weft is woven with two or more warp threads, which creates a dense, rugged cloth with a texture that works well as a background or for detailed pieces. There are several fabric companies that produce entire lines of denim fabric in both single colors and prints.

note: I like to upcycle when possible. Who doesn't have a tattered pair of jeans they no longer wear? Cut those up and use the fabric! When you are stitching with denim, you will notice that it has more stretch to it than chambray. Because it wants to stretch, you will need to tighten the fabric in your hoop frequently as you stitch if using denim as a background fabric.

WOOL

Wool fabric is most commonly made from the fibers of sheep's wool. It is denser than quilting cotton and does not have the drape of a knit fabric, which makes it a sturdy background for hoop art. It is an unexpected choice, and I love its texture and how it looks in a hoop. Because it is thicker than other fabrics you may be used to, it takes some practice securing it to the hoop.

Wool varies widely in both color and quality and is easily found in fabric stores. I like to search thrift stores for wool garments. These work very well when cut up for using in hoot art becuase the wool has often softened over time with wear.

FELT

Felt is usually made of wool or acrylic and can be readily found in craft and fabric stores. Wool felt is sold by the yard (found on bolts), and both wool and acrylic felt are sold in letter-size sheets or in 10" squares. One of the best features of felt is that it does not fray. For this reason, it is perfect for appliqués. I advise you to use wool felt rather than acrylic. I find that it has better hand, or drape, and a more substantial texture. Wool felt does not stretch as much as acrylic felt would. Acrylic felt is incredibly inexpensive, though, and is a fine choice if you need only a little for small details to add depth to your hoops.

selecting fabric prints

This is the fun part! Finding the perfect fabrics for your hoop art really defines the whole focus of your projects. Remember that your embroidery can add additional colors too.

USING BLACK AND WHITE FABRICS

Once you have spent the time putting together your ideal color palette, try removing all the colors and starting fresh with just black and white. Pick one additional color to go with that palette and choose several hues of thread in that color. Add a metallic or variegated thread. This will create monochromatic depth and makes an interesting statement piece.

I used this technique in this oval hoop (below), with black chambray as a background and a black and white floral print as my centerpiece. I chose neutral threads in gold, tan, and brown to embroider this piece.

USING LOW-VOLUME FABRICS

Now, let's remove just the black from the black and white palette we created and introduce low-volume colors back into it. Low-volume colors have a high concentration of white. They are not strictly white fabrics, though. A print fabric can be considered low-volume, such as a white fabric with orange and pink details. There are no hard and fast rules on what is considered to be a low-volume fabric, so don't feel hemmed in or anxious about it. Choose what you like! Restraint is key when the fabrics are "quiet." It can be surprising what stands out.

In this low-volume-inspired hoop, you'll see the background I chose is patterned and has several other colors, including metallic, besides white.

USING PRINTS

When you are choosing an outfit, you probably avoid mixing and matching busy patterns and prints. However, when you are creating a hoop, it is as if you are creating a whimsical, snow-globe world, free from the "rules" you give yourself when choosing clothing. Have fun with pattern! Layer a floral on top of another floral. Choose a busy background. You may reveal a whole new level of beauty when you throw pattern rules by the wayside! In this patterned hoop, I chose two busy fabrics that at first glance might not look like they match. However, when you take away the teal background from the flower print and add it to a completely different background, look how seamlessly the fabrics blend together. When you have an image that you want to highlight like this, cut as close as you can around the image to give it a seamless appearance when you place it on your background fabric. This technique is known as 'broderie perse' (see page 84).

MIXING TEXTURES

If you have dabbled in garment sewing, you know that blending fabrics of different weights can be tricky! In hoop art, although you certainly can create something lovely with one type of fabric, since both the appliqué and the stitching will add depth, I recommend layering fabrics of different weight to add even more texture to the finished piece.

One of the beauties of creating hoop art is that you do not have to take into consideration how different types of fabric will mix. If you like how it looks, that is all that matters and you are ready to begin! Consider using a textured fabric, like denim, with a quilting weight cotton and then adding jersey knit appliqués. When you combine embroidery with this unexpected combination of fabrics, you will create a piece of art that pops.

try this!: Instead of using scissors, rip the fabric into strips. This will result in uneven strips of fabric with frayed edges. This technique adds texture and a rustic appearance when using a solid or patterned fabric.

CHAPTER 4

Let's Talk About

STITCHING IN THE ROUND

simple hoop CONSTRUCTION

This method of assembling a hoop is the basis for creating simple hoop art–similar to the master recipe in a cookbook. From this point on, you will utilize this same process any time you create hoop art. Once you feel comfortable with thse steps, your ideas for creating will be limitless.

1. Begin by selecting two fabrics: a background fabric and a fabric that will be the focus of your hoop art (the main fabric). My main fabric is a panel from The Adventurers, a fabric by Cori Dantini. I chose a background fabric that closely matches the colors in the little boy's outfit, which I planned to embellish with stitching.

2. Choose a hoop size based on your main fabric. I chose a 12" hoop because I want to include the boy on the boat and also the reeds. Compare several hoop sizes on your fabric to be sure that you have the best fit. The appliqué that I chose could fit into a 10" hoop, but using the next size up prevents the image from feeling squashed into that smaller space.

Tip: If you want to paint or stain your hoop (see page 26), this is when you will do that. Allow enough time for the paint or stain to dry before continuing to the next step.

3. Loosen the screws at the top of the hoop and separate the two pieces. The hoop section with the screw on the top will be on the front of the fabric, and the hoop without any hardware will be behind the fabric.

4. Place the fabric between the front and back pieces of the hoop. Pull the fabric snug and begin to secure the hoop onto the background fabric by tightening the screws. Continue to pull

A GHASTLIE HOOP

This hoop was made using the Simple method; however, I stepped it up a notch and used two fabrics as the background. I picked out colors from Alexander Henry's "The Ghastlies" fabric that I wanted to highlight as my background. The background fabrics are by Cotton + Steel. I sewed them together using my sewing machine before I placed the family figures onto the fabric. By using a second fabric, the pink with gold metallic dots, I was able to mimic a floor that the family would then be standing on. Seaming two fabrics together is an easy way to add additional colors and design elements to your background fabric.

try this!

Construct a simple hoop using two pieces of fabric. To your main fabric, add several types of embroidery stitches until you cannot tell if it is a piece of fabric or a textured element as the focus of your hoop.

RAINY DAY

Banish the notion that just because this method of construction is called "simple", that your stitches must be kept simple as well. This hoop is made using just two pieces of fabric. The simplicity of the design allowed me to add a lot of additional colors through my embroidery. I used several different stitches on this hoop. When I was finished, the girl and her umbrella were no longer just a flat element on the background fabric. Instead, she stood apart from it and became the focus.

collage hoop CONSTRUCTION

Once you have mastered the construction of a simple hoop (see page 64), it's time to move on to the next step in hoop art: making a collage hoop. Making a collage hoop is much like making a simple hoop, except that you will be using more fabric elements than just a background fabric and a main fabric.

When you construct a fabric collage, your goal is to create a piece of art that feels cohesive. You can't give unnecessary worry to whether you are following color rules or if your fabrics match perfectly. You are the artist for this hoop. If you are happy and feel that the design works, then it works. It is as simple as that. This can be liberating but can also feel a little scary at first. By pushing yourself to mix and match elements on the small canvas of a hoop, I am confident you will come to embrace the freedom that comes with creating a design of your own. I like to think of this method as creating a fancier version of the collages that I made when I was in elementary school. When I was in fifth grade, our classroom had a complimentary subscription to USA Today. It was the highlight of my day to walk into the classroom and see a pile of crisp newspapers sitting on my teacher's desk, knowing that I would be given a section of that newspaper to cut up and create something new on a blank sheet of paper. Or maybe you are a scrapbooker at heart, and you have boxes of photos sitting alongside your specialty papers and stickers and trims. Either way, this method allows freedom of design.

1. Begin by choosing your hoop size and background fabric, just like you did with the simple hoop. I chose fabrics from two different lines by Carrie Bloomston's "Paint and Story".

> **Tip:** *Remember that if you want to paint or stain your hoop, this is when you will do that step (see page 26). Allow the hoop to dry before placing it on your fabric.*

2. Next decide on the placement of the background fabric in your hoop. Place the fabric in between the front and back pieces of the hoop and tighten the screw while pulling the fabric taut. A side benefit of tightening the fabric inside the hoop is that it begins to take on the shape of the hoop, which will be helpful when you begin to iron the pieces to your collage. Trim the fabric around your hoop to a width of approximately 1½" to 2" and set aside.

3. Choose the fabrics that you would like to use in your collage. I chose three fabrics from three separate fabric lines. Look at the fabrics and decide which elements you want to cut out

FREEHAND APPLIQUE

The fun part of creating a collage is that you can base it on your personal taste and interests. I really like coffee, and I decided to use a coffee cup in my collage. I based this design element on the shape of one of my favorite coffee cups (the cup design is in the pattern portion of the book on page 115).

If you want to include a special shape from a pattern as a design element in your collage, use a lightbox or the window method (see page 29) to trace your pattern.

To have the cups facing in opposite directions, I placed the pattern in one direction and traced it; then I flipped the pattern over and traced it once again.

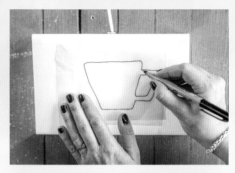

to use in your collage. I chose to cut out several flowers, leaves, words, and design elements from the fabric.

4. Once you have decided, cut the shapes from the fabric, leaving about 1" around your chosen pieces as done in the Simple method. It helps to cut out more than you think you need so you will have the chance to play around with the placement of the shapes on the fabric. You can decide as you create the collage which elements to use.

5. Following the manufacturer's directions, attach HeatnBond to your shapes. Do not peel the backing off just yet. You don't want to risk accidentally ironing your pieces in place before you've decided where you want them.

6. Begin working with the placement of your design elements. Shift things around until you are happy with the way your collage looks, then trim away any excess fabric from your elements.

7. Peel off the paper backing and iron each piece in place. With a collage-style hoop, it is best to iron pieces individually so that you can be sure of their correct placement on the hoop.

8. Choose the thread type and colors that you want to use for your hoop. For a busier pattern, you can tie everything together with a solid color stitch around every element. That will unify the pattern and from there you can add other colors and embroidery stitches. You will notice that I did this in my hoop. There are so many colors and shapes and design elements, that I chose to outline everything in shades of gray. From there I moved on to highlighting other areas with threads in various colors.

9. When you have finished stitching, complete your hoop following Steps 14–15 in the simple hoop assembly instructions (see page 67).

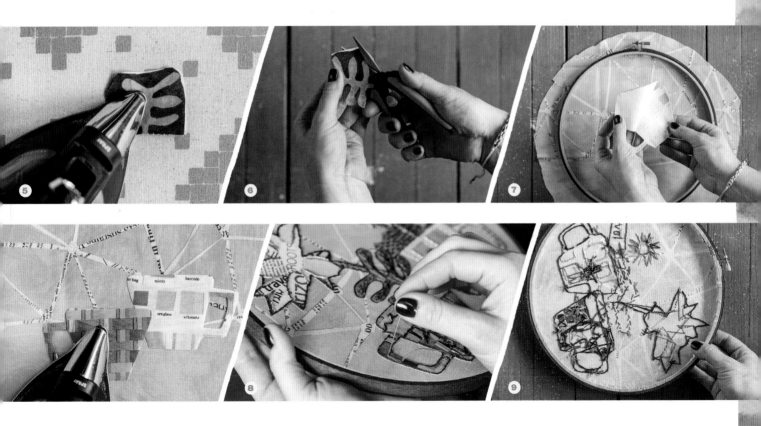

COLLAGE HOOPS

WONDERLAND BLOOMS

A collage-style hoop is a great way to pick out your favorite elements from an entire line of fabric; I chose Katarina Roccella's Wonderland line for this hoop. I couldn't decide which fabric I liked best, so I wanted to include some of everything. I began with a light-colored background. I wanted this to be lighter than the individual pieces, which are grays and blacks. As in my Ghastlie hoop (see page 69), I wanted to create a floor for my character to stand on, so I chose several selvage edges. You'll also notice that I added the word "Wonderland" from the selvage to a tree on the background. As manufacturers become more creative with these edges, these can be fun to use. From there, I put the rest of the hoop together by mixing and matching the pieces that I had cut until I was happy with the result. I added touches of an unexpected color in the stitching, and the result is a cohesive piece of art that makes me happy. If you achieve the same end result, I call that a success!

try this!

Try choosing fabrics from several designers and fabric lines. Push yourself to try to match colors or patterns when they aren't easily laid out for you, as they are in one line of fabric. Decide to choose fabrics that are all geometry based or that are all batiks or that are all in the same color family. Or choose a theme based on a place that inspires you. Giving yourself a challenge like this can result in creating something unexpected and exciting!

GEOMETRIC NATURE

For this hoop, I used a solid background which allows you to focus on aspects of the design while leaving some blank space. When I first started placing butterflies and flowers on this hoop, the geometric print was along the bottom but as I worked with the placement of the objects, I felt that by turning it on its side. This placement still had geometric interest, but it felt more playful and worked as an abstract part of the design. When creating a collage hoop, try something out of your ordinary comfort zone and you may be pleasantly surprised by what you create.

NEON GEMS

For this hoop, I chose to work with fabric from just one designer, Lizzy House. "Pearl Bracelets" is in the background and the gems from her "Natural History" fabric line is layerd on top. If you look at a full cut of the fabric, the gems are scattered throughout. I wanted to showcase some of my favorite gems but also have them fit within one hoop so I cut several gems and layerd them. I was able to fit everything into one hoop and make something new with the gems. Many novelty fabrics have elements like this that may be scattered about throughout the fabric. Try cutting out your favorites and combining them to the shape of a hoop and see what fun (and new!) combinations that you can create.

SURVIVORSHIP

CHAPTER 5

STITCHING OUTSIDE THE HOOP

making JEWELRY!

What outfit doesn't need a statement piece of jewelry? And even better — a statement piece of jewelry that you made for yourself. I love the mini-hoop necklace frames that Australian maker Dandelyne (see Resources, page 114) has created. They are ideal for making wearable embroidery pieces. If you feel that larger hoop art is an intimidating place to start, consider beginning with this smaller scale of embroidery.

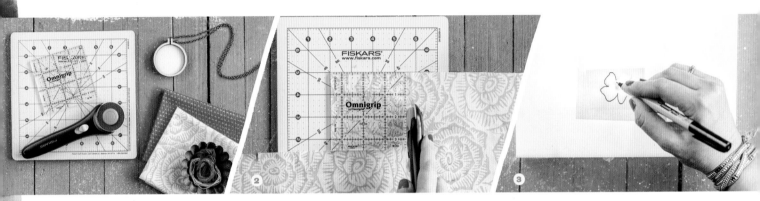

Gather your materials:

Dandelyne mini-hoop necklace

2 fabric choices

3½" square ruler (or small square ruler that has ½" markings)

Cutting mat

Rotary cutter

Micro-tip scissors

HeatnBond

Iron

White all-purpose glue

1. I used a flower pattern that I designed to fit a 2" mini-hoop necklace. Based on the size of your necklace, reduce or enlarge the pattern (see page 121) as needed. Or create a pattern of your own.

2. Choose one of your fabrics to be the background fabric. Using a square ruler that is approximately 2" larger than your hoop, a cutting mat and a rotary blade, cut a square of the background fabric. Set aside.

3. Using a lightbox or a window and a pen or pencil, trace your correctly sized pattern onto a small piece of HeatnBond.

4. Place your traced HeatnBond pattern piece onto the back side of the second fabric. Adhere with an iron. Before touching, wait several seconds for this piece to cool. Then cut out the piece using micro-tip scissors. Remove the paper backing.

5. Place your background fabric on the ironing board and on top of that position your cut-out piece of fabric. It helps to place your necklace on the fabric as well, so that you can have accurate placement. When you are happy with how it looks, carefully remove the necklace frame and iron the pattern piece in place.

Tip: It is important to note for the next step that I normally do not recommend stitching without a hoop. On larger projects your embroidery stitches need the tension that a hoop provides. However, for mini pieces of fabric like this, I always stitch without a hoop, using my fingers to control the tension while I stitch. It may take a bit of practice to adjust to this way of stitching, but continue to practice and soon this method will feel natural.

6. You are ready to stitch! Choose your threads and a needle. Begin with an outline stitch on the accent fabric. A necklace does get a lot of wear and the outline stitch ensures that the fabric will remain firmly in place.

7. When you have finished embellishing with embroidery, place your necklace frame back on the fabric. At this point, follow the manufacturer's directions that came with your mini-hoop for placing the fabric in the hoop and tightening the necklace.

8. Use white all-purpose glue to adhere the edges of the fabric to the back of the necklace. Once the glue is dry, refer to the directions and add the back piece.

9. Now for the most important part: Choose an outfit carefully! You are displaying your time and effort and beautiful handiwork for everyone to see. Wear it proudly!

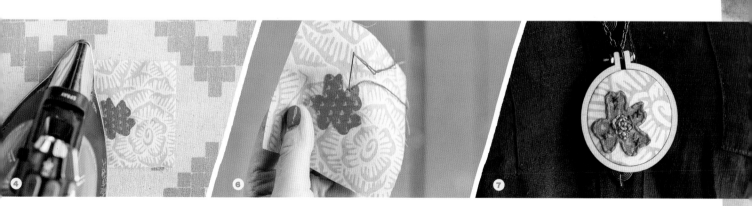

WEARABLES & ACCESSORIES

Once you have created a few projects "in the round," you'll soon realize that you are not limited to creating art that can only be displayed on the walls throughout your house. The embroidery and fabric-layering skills that you have been honing can be used in any number of other projects.

Clothing, whether a casual jean and T-shirt combo or a dressier skirt and top combo, can take on your unique style depending on how you choose to embellish them. And, no, we're not talking about gaudily adding jewels to your clothes! I chose two projects to show you how much fun it can be to add your personal, tasteful style to a piece of ready-made clothing. But don't stop there! You can Boho-up other elements of your wardrobe: bags, scarves, even buttons.

THE CLASSIC WHITE SHIRT

A white shirt can go with nearly anything, but I decided to up the ante and make this white shirt worthy of running fancy errands around town!

This is the perfect example of tone-on-tone appliqué and embroidery. I wanted the shirt to have just a hint of appliqué, so I chose to go with white on white. I used these Cotton + Steel webs as a floral motif. By cutting out each "flower" individually and then arranging them in a cascading pattern, it no longer looks like a spider web, which is how the fabric was originally styled.

I added a small touch of color through the embroidery thread. This Sue Spargo Razzle embellishment thread is 100% rayon and has a lovely silky feel to it. It adds a touch of shimmer and, because it is variegated, it adds a variety of color in white, ivory, and pale peach. I kept the stitches simple and made sure they were secure enough to stay put during washing and wearing.

JEANS, JEANS, JEANS

These aren't the embellished jeans of the 1970s! With a little (okay, more than a little) help from Shannon of Googiemomma, we created a bevy of jeans worthy of adoration from the littlest member of her clan, yet cool enough for her teenage daughter to swoon over.

If you can make a collage hoop (see page 68), then this will be an easy next step to take your work outside of the hoop. Begin by cutting out the design elements from a fabric that you like. We chose to mix and match several Cotton + Steel fabrics to form an entirely new look.

You will add your HeatnBond to the pieces, just like you do when you create a hoop and then arrange your pieces onto the denim and iron them on. Embellish with embroidery to finish.

Tip: When ironing quilting cotton to denim, it may take more ironing than when you are just adhering a cotton piece to a cotton background. Until the fabric pieces have been secured with stitches, they may want to move around. Be patient and have an iron at the ready while you are embroidering!

PURSES, BAGS AND POUCHES

If you like to make your own bags out of fabrics you love, then take that care one step further and create an appliquéd design to embroider onto your project. This project is the Sew Together Pouch, which was created by SewDemented and is available for purchase on Craftsy — although any bag or pouch pattern can be embellished in this way. I collaborated with Jade of Stitchmischief, who has incomparable bag-sewing skills and an amazing array of colorful zippers!

I chose "Blueberry Park" fabrics by Karen Lewis for this bag. You'll notice that I used a yellow floral print cut from one of her fabrics. For the other two flowers I created my own flower pattern based on the look of the yellow flower. You can copy this idea by using the design in the pattern section of this book (see page 115), or create a floral pattern all your own.

try this!

Isolate an image from a piece of fabric that you like and create a bag or pouch based around that design. Choose the colors and fabrics and stitches that will enhance the design you created!

SMALLER PROJECTS

If you want to add a hint of Boho style to your wardrobe, but you aren't ready to take the leap into embellishing your clothes, I suggest starting with a small project, like this beautiful scarf.

I found this drapey knit scarf at a secondhand store and snatched it up for this project. For an accessory like this, one that has a well-worn feel to it, I chose to use a knit fabric rather than quilting cotton. It is important to consider the fabric that you are using as your background when you are choosing your embellishment fabrics. The knit feathers add to the design of the striped scarf without weighing it down with a fabric that doesn't flow. I stiched threads in brighter colors to add to the design and draw attention to the feathers lightly falling down the scarf.

Normally, I do not worry much about what the stitches look like on the back of a project. I like to see the business of the threads intertwined into random and colorful patterns when I am done stitching. I also do not knot my threads; I simply twist them through other threads to secure them. However, with a project like this scarf, it is likely that both the front and back will be seen at times. When I am stitching an article of clothing, I pay more attention to what my stitches look like from both sides.

When I don't want messy stitches from behind to detract from the cool design and stitches on the front, I tie a small knot in my stitches when I have finished with whatever thread I am using. This makes for a neater look, and for a project that will be repeatedly washed and worn, it's nice to know that I have properly secured my threads and they shouldn't unravel during use.

FABRIC-COVERED BUTTONS

Fabric-covered buttons are a versatile, and often overlooked, accessory that can be used for many things besides clothing. They can be tucked into the wrapping of a small package to personalize a gift. And with the right tools, they can even be turned into Boho-styled hair slides. I like to use an aluminum cover button kit for making fabric-covered buttons. You can also use these kits to make jewelry! Tailor my directions for assembling and stitching a mini-hoop necklace on page 76 according to the instructions and circular templates in your button kit. With the included circular templates, you will know exactly how much fabric you need to cut for your buttons. The button kits come with a mix of button backs or flat backs. Button backs are perfect for … (you guessed it) buttons! Flat backs have a variety of uses. For example, if you finish your buttons with the flat backs, you can add a small magnet to the back of the button and create lovely and useful magnets for your refrigerator or office space. Color-code them to help you keep track of important items on your to-do list.

EMBELLISHING HOOP ART

Another use for the flat backs and magnets is to create a needle minder that you can attach to your hoop to keep track of your needle as you work. If you have ever had the experience of losing your needle while switching threads, you will appreciate a needle minder! To make one of these, place one of your lovely embellished magnets on one side of the fabric in your hoop and another on the back of the fabric. Picture it like a sandwich: the magnets are the bread, and the fabric of your hoop is whatever deliciousness is inside your sandwich. The magnet will mind your needle whenever you need to put it down. Make several needle minders and tuck them into gifts for your crafty friends. Just don't forget to keep one for yourself!

BOHO HAIR SLIDES

You can also use these small flat-backed buttons to make coordinating Boho hair slides to coordinate with your outfits. By attaching a hair slide with a flat pad at the end to your button, you will create a unique fashion accessory that can be the finishing touch to your outfit.

INSPIRED BY: *english paper piecing*

Have you fallen for English paper piecing yet? I would say try it once and you'll be hooked, but it took me a little longer than that to fall head over heels in love with this relaxing (and addicting!) form of handiwork.

Templates for English paper piecing can be purchased, all packaged up and ready to use. They are typically made of a reusable material like plastic or a thick card stock. Templates can also be found online in a variety of sizes, which you then can print onto card stock using your printer. Or you can create your own shapes by tracing shapes onto card stock or thin cardboard, like a cereal box.

Once you have your templates cut out, it is just a matter of picking fabric and hand basting your pieces. Continue basting your pieces until you have a few thousand and then you can make a quilt! Or for instant gratification, baste a few pieces and sew them together to display in a hoop as a piece of art. I have not had the patience to create the thousand or so hexies (or other forms of English paper piecing) needed to make something large, but I do enjoy looking at my scaled-down handiwork in a hoop.

The hoop on the left in the photograph opposite, was created by someone whom I consider to be an English paper piecing maven: Rhea of Alewives Fabrics. Just walking into her fabric shop in Damariscotta Mills, Maine, is an inspiration of color and fabrics — and once you see the hand-pieced inspiration gracing the walls, you will want to become an English paper piecing maven as well.

This is a true English paper pieced hoop, pieced together with 1" elongated hexagons, also called honeycombs. Once Rhea created a background fabric the width of the hoop, she adhered a floral motif in the center and embroidered that piece. This is a great example of how you can tailor a background fabric to your liking. By piecing together small sections of fabrics in this way, you are creating a larger piece of fabric that is completely your own.

I made the second hoop on the right in the photograph opposite, using a mock–English paper piecing method. You will still need a template, but your template will be traced onto HeatnBond and then transferred onto the fabric. Cut out your paper-backed pieces and arrange them in a pattern on your background fabric. Carefully iron the pieces in place one at a time to avoid shifting pieces of fabric and creating lines that do not match up.

I first adhered my pieces in place and embellished them with embroidery stitches. Then I traced the pentagon flower and reduced it in size on my printer and used a Karisma mechanical pencil to trace the flower onto the fabric between the paper pieced flowers. I used a backstitch in the same color as the background fabrics to add tone-on-tone color interest.

INSPIRED BY: *novelty fabric*

There are so many adorable novelty fabrics that are sure to grab your attention. With a little fussy cutting and imagination, you can turn that novelty fabric into a piece of art unique to your style.

For this fabric-inspired hoop, I first saw the fabric and then the hoop design came to me. I used Lila's Kitchen fabric by Makower UK. When I first saw this kitschy kitchen fabric, complete with vintage tea kettles and mugs, miniature radios, and tiny spice bottles, I immediately pictured a retro kitchen in colors of avocado green, harvest gold, and cerulean blue, much like the colors of the kitchen in my childhood home.

I sketched a simple kitchen design, chose the elements from the fabric that I wanted to include in my hoop, and cut and ironed them in place. The kitchen was further embellished with embroidery, and voila, a vintage kitchen!

Create your own design based on an element from a novelty fabric that catches your eye. It does not have to be complicated. Maybe you want to create a woodland scene using a fabric printed with owls, bears, and foxes, or maybe you want to create a beach scene with fabric printed with sailboats and lighthouses. Pick a fabric with designs that you like and create your hoop from there.

CHAPTER 7

×××××××××××

Let's Talk About

THRIFTING
FOR OLD
TREASURES

Has the thrifting bug bitten you yet? It can be satisfying to find exactly what you are looking for when you go to a thrift or antique store or even a yard sale. More often than not, however, you don't find what you are looking for right away. Patience is required when you decide to use vintage goods in your embroidery projects. I can't tell you how many thrift stores I have visited over and over again until I found what I wanted for the projects in this section.

I am always in pursuit of hoops, obviously. Really sturdy, old hoops. And bonus if they are German made! Older hoops are made of better quality materials and sturdier hardware, and they rarely splinter. The newer hoops are certainly functional, but you can see a visible difference when they are held side-by-side with finely crafted vintage hoops. Have I mentioned that you should snatch up those old hoops when you can find them? Maybe. But snatch them up you should!

When thrifting, I'm also on the lookout for linens: tea towels, tablecloths, pillowcases, handkerchiefs, wool blazers and skirts. Anything that can be used as a foundation for a new piece of art. Fabric found in this way can usually be purchased a lot cheaper than if you were to buy it new. Plus, you are giving used items a new life! Doesn't that make you feel great?

My favorite part of thrifting is the story. There is always a story behind the items you find. You may not know that story, but once it becomes yours, the item gets a brand-new story: "I have been looking for linens just like my grandmother had and used for our family get-togethers when I was a small child." Or, "I have been searching for this exact Pyrex pattern and scored this one at a yard sale for two dollars!" There is always a story, and the new story that you give your find makes it even more special.

OLD FRAMES

I visited a new-to-me antique mall, and this frame was the first item I happened upon. Coming in at $4 and with just the right amount of well-worn spots around the edges, it was just the thing to work into a piece of embroidery. I combined it with a silver metallic and yellow background and thought it had the right proportions to mimic an old family portrait. Not a family portrait to grace the halls of Downton Abbey, perhaps, but more like one you would find on the walls of your quirky aunt Violet's house. This "Mister Stache" fabric from Alexander Henry (see opposite) was ideal for creating the portrait.

In most instances, it works best to stitch this project in an embroidery hoop and then transfer it from the hoop to a backing board and then to the frame. Glue or staple the fabric to the backing board, much like you would adhere a project to a piece of canvas. The back of the project is rarely seen, so as long as the project is secured and wrinkle free from the front, it doesn't much matter what the back looks like.

And remember, you can always add a thin piece of felt to the back to cover up your stitches and make it gift-worthy.

RETRO TABLECLOTHS

I do not entertain nearly enough to warrant having a drawer full of tablecloths. A handful of well-loved vintage tablecloths is all I really need. However, when I saw this mustard yellow tablecloth in pristine condition at a nearby thrift store, reduced to $2.50 from the $5 price tag, I decided right then that I must have it. I bought it and ran, in case they realized the treasure they were letting me get away with! If you find a tablecloth with a motif that you like, definitely snatch it up. It might pain you to cut into a vintage piece of linen like this, but just think of it as a really big piece of fabric that you are helping to preserve.

Because I wanted to update the feel of this while keeping it kitschy, I decided to choose a vibrant purple background fabric made up of macramé stitches by Rashida Coleman-Hale. The macramé designs on the background suited the '70s-style pitcher and flowers from the tablecloth, and the grape color, although not found in the original tablecloth, elevated the style of this hoop to a modern-day vibe.

For a modern painted look, I chose to embroider wide straight stitches in a random pattern on the vase and flowers. I felt like this needed to have the appearance of a quick sketch using pens and paints. It was fun to not be so precise with my stitches and instead to use long lines of colors and stitches and place them where they looked right. It felt as if I were painting with wide brushstrokes of thread.

Try creating a project in which you do not need small, tidy stitches but can instead work with your needle and thread like a painter would work with a brush and broad strokes of paint. Do not over-think the embroidery process on a project like this. Step back from it occasionally, as you would a painting, to ensure it is taking on the appearance that you want.

FEED SACKS

Vintage feed sacks, although faded, can have delightfully charming images to use in your embroidery. I found this feed sack hanging toward the back of a very cold antique warehouse. I had passed by several, very faded and very pricey, feed sacks before I spotted this cheeky little rooster. It was not a complete sack, which probably justified the low $10 price, but I knew it would be ideal for creating a rustic feed sack–themed hoop.

I took the scissors to this one only after much deliberation. I decided to use just a few elements from the original sack. As a background, I chose Maude Asbury's "Luckie" fabric, which replicates a bandana pattern. I then cut out the rooster and added him to the fabric. I used the mock–English paper piecing method and the pattern on page 115 to cut words in coffin shapes, which I added underneath the rooster. A thin strip of leather-like trim was embroidered using the couching stitch. I tried to keep the feel of the vintage feed sack while updating it, and I picture it being right at home in a farmhouse kitchen. Also on my list of things to find!

Enjoy the thrill of the chase while looking for just the right thrifted items that will allow you to practice your new embroidery and design skills! Start small and with items that are not pricey. Cloth napkins and handkerchiefs can be used in a perfect starter project that will allow you to showcase your skills without feeling like you are cutting up an heirloom and priceless piece of fabric. Think outside of the hoop and choose items that will fit well with your decor.

LIVE A
COLORFUL
LIFE

VINTAGE TEA TOWELS

The majority of tea towels that I find are stained and wrinkled from years of daily use. It is not often that I come across a pristine tea towel that retains the feel of an antique linen. So when I discovered this crisp white towel, with the perfect coral colored stripes running from top to bottom and the $2 price tag, I picked it up even though I did not have a definite plan for it. Sometimes you have to put things away for a rainy day, because you never know when you will find such a great vintage item again.

I wanted to make something outside of the hoop for this project, so I decided on a wall hanging. A wall hanging would allow me to appreciate the tea towel in all its vintage glory, but it also was a decent-size clean slate, that allowed me to have fun coming up with a design. I chose to use a combination of three fabrics from Riley Blake's "Fancy and Fabulous" line, which incorporates black and white vintage style-sketches and floral prints. I incorporated elements from all three fabrics and made a fabric collage. I chose to hand sew a hem at the top with a row of decorative stitches for a dowel to fit through, but if you can find an old wooden hanger, it would have an equally charming effect while keeping true to the antique feel of the project.

✕ ✕ ✕ ✕ ✕ ✕ ✕ ✕ ✕ ✕

CHAPTER 8

Let's Talk About

STITCHING WHAT YOU SEE

try this! Look to nature for inspiration and create one additional design to go alongside these three patterns. Choose a palette that is reminiscent of colors you would find in nature or go in the opposite direction and choose unexpected colors that would not normally be found on these objects in nature. For a fun twist, use neons!

At this point, you know how to put together a hoop using fabrics that you like and want to combine. You have found inspiration in quilt patterns and art books and have learned how to Boho up your wardrobe. You have all the tools you need to continue creating. Now it's time to take the reins and create something that is entirely your own using some of my prompts here as inspiration.

To illustrate these prompts, I will walk you through several projects that I created using design elements and items that I am personally inspired by. There is nothing like the satisfaction of creating a design on paper from an idea in your head and then transferring that into a fabric design that you can hold in your hands and embroider! For each of my patterns, I will give you a suggestion of how to create something that is tailored to your interests, so that you can feel the same satisfaction that comes from creating.

For all these patterns, you will use the method of first tracing the pattern onto HeatnBond and then transferring that to fabric (see page 25).

try this! *Use the patterns on pages 123-125 rather than collaged designs. Trace a design directly onto a piece of fabric using the lightbox/window method (see page 28) and a heat-erasable or water-soluble pen. Simply embellish this design with embroidery stitches in various thread weights and colors.*

LOOK TO NATURE

Inspiration from nature can come from anything outside your door. It can be as simple as a small stack of stones, a snowflake, a feather, or a leaf. Do not overly complicate the designs that you find in nature. There is so much symmetry in nature already. It is easy to use your inspirational object and divide it according to its own inherent geometry to create an abstract design. Or draw it true-to-life and add texture and details with your fabric and thread. This is about your creativity, so you can be as simplistic or detailed as you want to be in your drawing and stitching. Use a variety of fabrics to mimic the colors found in nature.

The first trio of patterns I created can be seen in the photograph oposite. I love happening upon small stacks of rocks. My son loves rocks of all sorts, and I find piles of them everywhere outside the house (and often inside, too!). I also love feathers. I love their colors and patterns and texture, so I am constantly inspired by them. The geometric nature of a tree is simple and fun to create with a variety of fabrics.

I display them on three narrow canvas forms. To do this, remove your stitched fabric from the embroidery hoop, place it on a canvas and trim the excess fabric (leaving enough to wrap around the back of the canvas). Use a staple gun to attach the finished project onto the canvas. Take your time and be sure that your fabric is pulled taut, without leaving bunches or wrinkles on the front part of the canvas. You can reduce or enlarge the patterns to suit whatever project you decide to create.

LOOKING AT TRENDS

What is currently a popular trend in decorating? Are foxes and owls found on everything from clothing to decorative items for the nursery? Is minimalism the barely-there trend that you can't get enough of? Do you like to mix galvanized metals with soft, feminine colors? Harness a popular style and create a piece of art that embraces what you love about that trend!

When I created this next group of designs (see patterns on pages 125-128), I was inspired by the influence of Native American patterns that seemed to be cropping up everywhere. I narrowed my ideas down to four designs that appealed to me most: a geometric pattern, the sun, an animal, and a feather.

This is a small, simple project that will give you a sense of satisfaction when you have finished, as if it took you eight hours to make. The small scale provides a great opportunity to practice the various stitches that became popular in crazy quilting: the herringbone (see page 41), feather (see page 43), and lazy daisy (see page 42) stitches!

try this! *Decide what trend is inspiring you and create a pattern celebrating it. Go outside of your color comfort zone and choose a palette that you do not typically work with. I like to look at color trends online and work with palettes that are becoming popular even if they are not my ideal ones. You might be surprised at what you come up with!*

LOOKING AT DESIGN

If the thought of creating a series of patterns based on nature or an animal seems daunting, this next prompt might be the project for you. What design elements appeal to you? What style do you gravitate toward when you decorate: traditional, industrial modern, mid-century modern, Scandinavian, Southwestern, Zen, nautical, rustic, farmhouse, cottage, Bohemian, or vintage? What style is resonating with you at the moment? Go with that.

Personally, I am intrigued by the resurgence of mid-century modern design. Items like vintage dinnerware, Eames furniture, starburst mirrors, bubble lighting fixtures, each are representative of this design style. But, I like combining some of the elements characteristic of mid-century modern design with my other favorite inspirational design styles to create a unique Scandinavian/Bohemian/rustic look. These styles all embody clean lines and minimalism, but it is the combination of many different influences that resonates with me and

creates truly personalized work. What unique combination of design styles best depicts you?

This pattern is so simple and yet embraces the elements of mid-century modern design that I love. I was watching North by Northwest while I sketched this design, and it has a vibe of tailored suits and martinis. Use a color palette like this, or select a different palette with a mix of solid and patterned fabrics.

try this! *Create a simple pattern based on a design element or period of time that you are drawn to. Look up the color palettes that were commonly used during the time period you are referencing and use that palette to complete your design.*

One of my favorite design styles is Scandinavian: a mix of nature, abstract designs, and bright colors. I created five designs (see pages 116-120) that have a Scandinavian feel to them. The beauty is that their elements are interchangeable. Together they make a thematic set, but each piece can also stand on its own.

For two of the hoops (the geometric heart and the floral pattern), I used only solid prints, and for the other three (the sectioned heart, the bird and rabbit floral, and the row of houses), I used only patterned fabrics. If you are making all five hoops as a set, decide on a color palette first and try to blend one or two of your chosen fabrics into every hoop. This will unify your hoops and will make them look like a complete set.

try this! *Mix and match! Add elements from one of the patterns in the book to another pattern and create an entirely new design. Use a photocopier to enlarge or reduce the patterns to modify the look of the design you want to create.*

LOOK AT HOME

What do you fill your space with? Are there designer shoes lined up neatly on shelves (and squirreled away under your bed and in your closet)? Do you collect vintage bowls and plates (you know who you are!)? Are your shelves (and your bedside table) stacked with piles of books (the finger is pointing at me!)? Look around your home for inspiration.

My home is filled with small terra-cotta pots of succulents. I can't keep other houseplants or garden plants alive, but I tend to my collection of succulents and somehow they thrive. I find so much inspiration in these little pots of spiky greenery. In the summer they are happy to be outside in the sun, but even in the cold and dark winters in the Northeast, here is a plant that will never die due to lack of sun. This is a design based on one of my very favorite (and thriving!) succulents that flowers during the winter.

try this! *Look around your home and decide what inspires you. Sketch a few simple designs and create a pattern based on those designs. Choose a color palette that matches your favorite room or a treasured item and make your fabric choices based on that. Try creating a series of patterns based on your original sketches.*

PATTERNS

Feed Sack Hoop

Sew Together Pouch

Fabric Collage

Scandinavian 1
(8" hoop)
Enlarge 125%

Scandinavian 2
(10" hoop)
Enlarge 150%

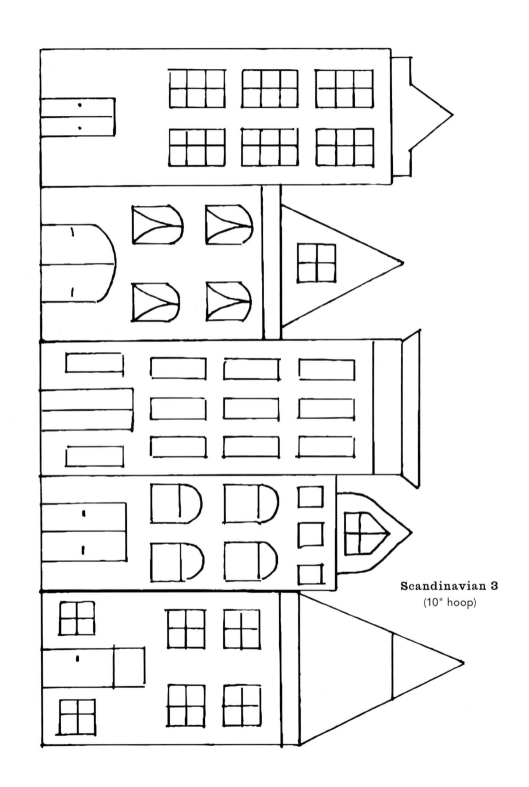

Scandinavian 3
(10" hoop)

Scandinavian 4
(10" hoop)
Enlarge 125%

Scandinavian 5
(8" hoop)
Enlarge 125%

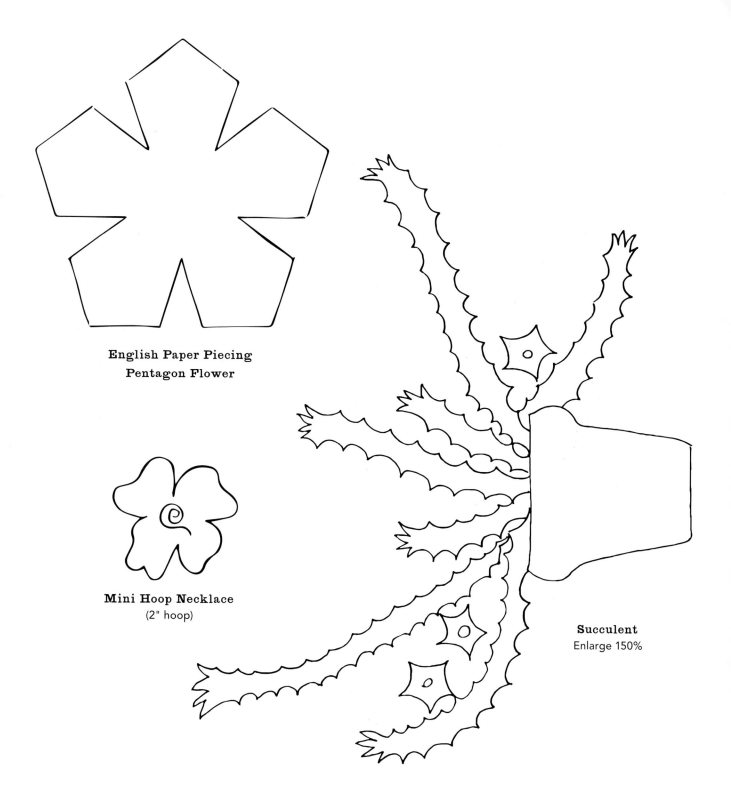

English Paper Piecing
Pentagon Flower

Mini Hoop Necklace
(2" hoop)

Succulent
Enlarge 150%

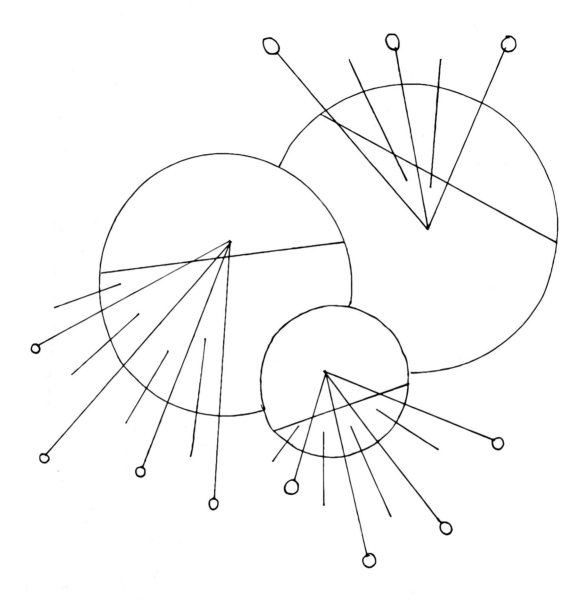

Mid-Century Modern
Enlarge 150%

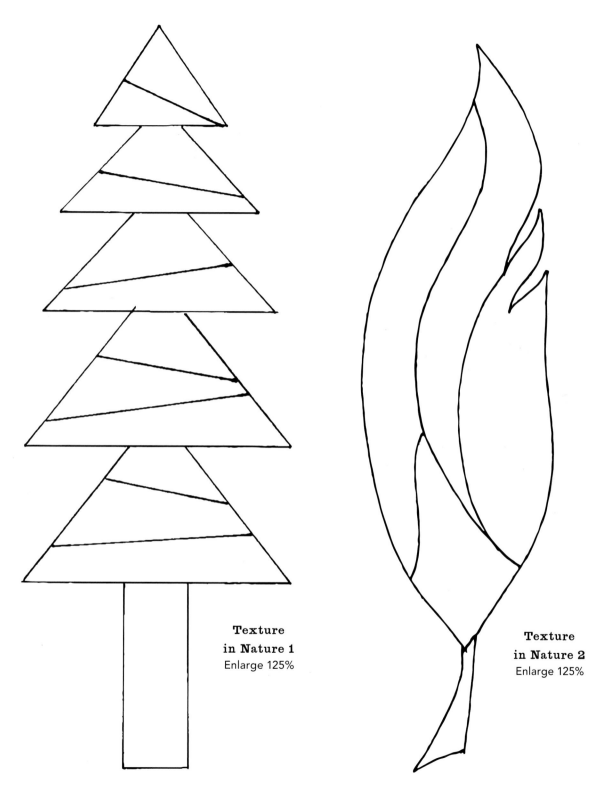

**Texture
in Nature 1**
Enlarge 125%

**Texture
in Nature 2**
Enlarge 125%

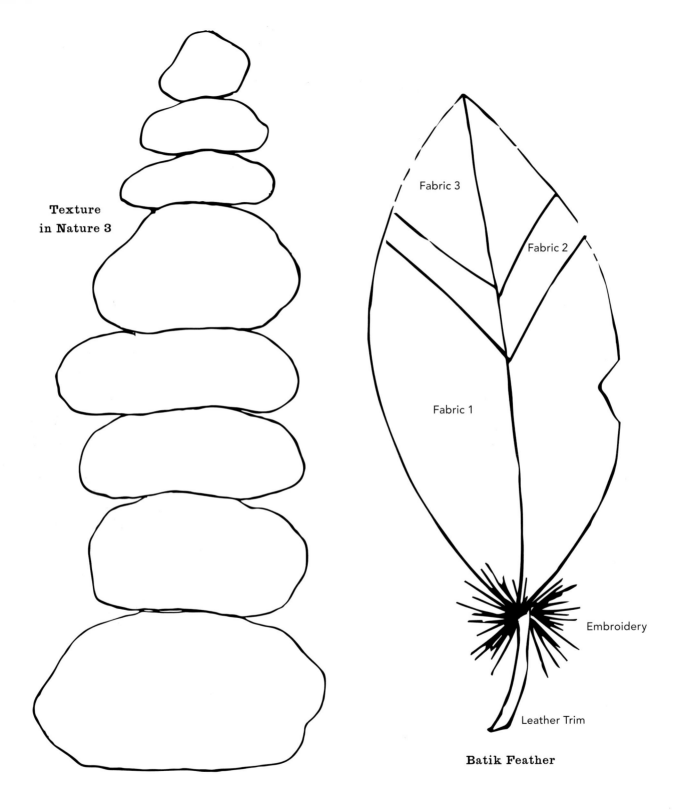

Texture in Nature 3

Fabric 3

Fabric 2

Fabric 1

Embroidery

Leather Trim

Batik Feather

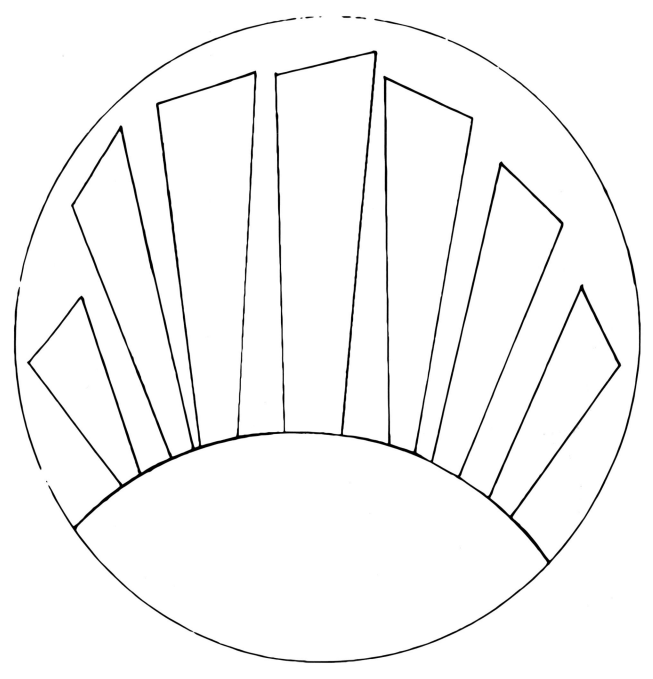

Native Boho 1
(7" hoop)

Native Boho 2
(7" hoop)

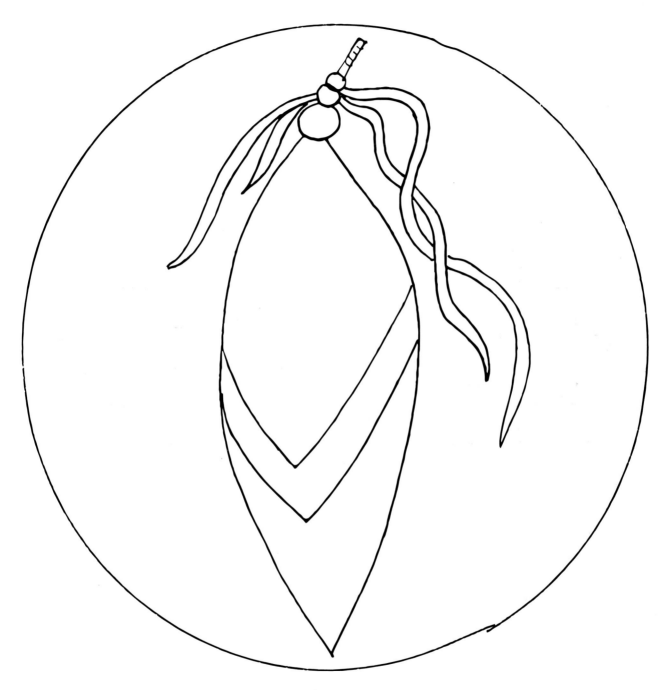

Native Boho 3
(7" hoop)

Native Boho 4
(7" hoop)